Discovery
AFTER A GALE
FORCE WIND

Jay Fox

20 Twenty
Literary Group

Jay Fox, Author
163 Drew Howard Rd, Crossville, TN 38558
Email: jayfox.fox290@gmail.com
Web: jayfoxbermuda.com

ISBN
978-1-961250-00-0 (Paperback)
978-1-961250-01-7 (eBook)

Discovery
AFTER A GALE
FORCE WIND

AUTHOR'S NOTE

This is a personal story about my triumph over the tragedy of the loss of my leg. Many of us, in the midst of adversity, and the storms of life, live in fear of uncertainty. Our life journey begins, wide and calm like a peaceful sea. There seems to be no trouble that we can see on the horizon. Then, suddenly the clouds move in. The winds begin to blow. They get stronger and stronger. The swells begin to rise, and we get tossed from side to side. Our thoughts begin to flow; will we perish or will we survive? In the midst of all our confusion, should we lose hope?

We ask ourselves, "What lies beyond this mystery of uncertainty?"

I believe that, in the journey that we travel, we should remain focused and faithful; the storms of life will pass...we will survive!

Jay Fox

Acknowledgements

I want to thank the ladies of The Write Touch, Inspirational Writers Group, Fairfield Glade, in Tennessee for encouraging me to tell my story, also Ruth Berkes and Mary Holyer Black for editing my drafts.

I, personally, want to thank the Lord for preserving my life, so I could tell my story.

Bermuda Archives

Original manuscripts form a rich repository of information concerning shipwrecks, Admirals, passenger lists, and much other material of Bermuda history. The material is readily accessible with microfilm viewing.

Some descriptions of storms in this book are from historical manuscripts, but most are from my personal imagination and experience.

Dedication

This story is dedicated to my wife Catherine and to my immediate family: daughters Julie, Rebecca and Jacqueline, my son Cameron and my step daughter Kimberly.

My grandchildren include Mycah, Ajai, Alia, Aidan, Ariah, Matthew, Ashley and Thomas...each a special treasure.

My greatest wish is that you will truly love God and triumph over all of your own tragedies.

ABOUT THE AUTHOR

Jay Fox

"I came to find my Jesus."

Jay Fox, Recording Artist and Song Evangelist, was born on the island of Bermuda Oct. 26, 1949. Much acclaimed for his 'feeling renditions.' Many who have heard him have remarked on the emotions he evokes in the audience as he paints a mood with his palette of songs. Jay's soft, easy- listening voice embraces God's message in all his music, whether a popular hit or his own composition, in an irresistible "Jay" manner.

Barbara Woodings, Writer

TABLE OF CONTENTS

THE JOURNEY

Jay's life journey began in the multicultural vacation paradise of Bermuda. It has a musical tradition as rich and beautiful as the island itself. In his secular music, the soulful rhythms that appeared in his romantic ballads appealed to a wide audience, where men and women of all ages appreciated the unique qualities found in his work. Just as the incoming tide gently flooded the coral reefs in Bermuda's Castle Harbor, Jay's voice also washed over his audience, exposing them to a wide range of emotions. Like other island entertainers, Jamaica's Harry Belafonte and Hawaii's Don Ho, Jay gave each of his listeners a memorable performance, which led to a long, successful career on the island. Jay realized, however, that, just as the incoming tide carried him to the top of his professional career on the island, the outgoing tide revealed something very important was missing from his life... God.

Jay spent most of his career performing in hotels and nightclubs, and, on several occasions, he used his talent to do benefit concerts for Bermuda's handicapped and the King Edward Memorial Hospital. He appeared on several local TV talk shows and Christmas shows. Jay also produced his own TV show, having special guest appearances and other local entertainers. On a few occasions, he travelled abroad as an agent of the Bermuda Department of Tourism to promote the Island. Then, one day, while attending a luncheon at a local church, his whole life changed: God spoke to him saying, *"I'm going to use your gift of singing to further my Kingdom."* Jay realized at that moment that God had been right beside him all along, and now He was leading him into a career of gospel singing.

By sharing his experience with his friends and colleagues, he has become a witness for what God can do in your life when you let Him in.

With the help of his experience as a performer, his study for the Ministry, scripture reading, sermons and the 'Still Small Voice' of God, Jay began writing and then recording Christian songs. Jay's personal journey, directed by that 'Still Small Voice,' led him from Bermuda to Tennessee. There, he sang gospel concerts every Sunday afternoon at Legends Dinner Theater in Crossville.

Jay is a member of The American Society of Composers, Authors and Publishers. In addition to his concerts, Jay has a distinguished recording career. He formed his Music Group of Companies - J. D. K. Fox, Music Group Inc., Manchester Music Makers, Treetop Productions, Orpheus Sound Recordings and Orpheus Music Ministry- to handle all of his recording work.

His first album, *Signature* was both an artistic and commercial success; it contained his own compositions as well as music by other island entertainers. *Signature* was followed by six other easy-listening albums: *Reflections, Christmas Classics, Island of Paradise, Jay Fox Live At the Princess, More Than Ever,* and *Something Special.* His latest projects have all been gospel music: *After the Sunset, It's My Desire, Jay Fox Live in Nashville,* and *Greater Faith featuring Jay Fox.*

His latest single *I Came to Find My Jesus* was released from his CD *After the Sunset.* It is regularly heard on Christian radio stations across the country.

Over the years as a songwriter, Jay has been inspired by writers like Bob Allen, writer of the classic Chances Are, sung by Johnny Mathis, and singers like Andy Williams, Perry Como, Harry Belafonte, Frank Sinatra and Elvis Presley. Today, Jay is inspired by some of the best inspirational writers in gospel music: Lanny Wolfe's

Surely the Presence of the Lord is in This Place, Joel Hemphill's *It Is No Secret* and Bill and Gloria Gaither's *Because He Lives.*

After singing in hotels for many years, he rededicated his life and his love of music and singing to promote the Gospel of Jesus Christ in word and song. He is now a Song Evangelist, for the Church of the Nazarene, East Tennessee District. Sunday mornings, when not singing at concerts, you can find Jay leading a Bible study or leading as Minister of Music in his local church. In addition to his concerts, he has given his time to present Bible studies weekly at Health and Rehabilitation Centers for seniors in Crossville, Tennessee.

Thousands of fans and friends Jay has made over the years have expressed that they feel blessed by his messages through music and song.

Randy Norris
Writer & Contributor
Crossville Chronicle, Tennessee.

BERMUDA

Romantic beaches, tall sailing ships and Buccaneers... allow me to share a little history about the island where I was born. I must point out that this is not a history book about Bermuda. However, some historical facts were retrieved from the Bermuda Archives. The archives are amongst the World's richest and most comprehensive. Dating back to the island's earliest settlers in the 1600s, the government's official records give a virtually uninterrupted accounting of the Islands' past. Many Bermudians use the archives to trace their family history.

Photo source unknown   Photo source unknown

Tall Ships around the world still reenact voyages of the past. As a young boy, I used to play at St. David's Lighthouse near my home. The voyagers who found the islands ended their journey at St. David's head; one of the many smaller islands of Bermuda.

One of Bermuda's former Governors, John Henry Lefroy, became Commander-in-Chief in 1871. He compiled information into two volumes called *Memorials of the Discovery* and *Early Settlement of Bermuda*. These Memorials constitute a remarkable dossier of colonial data, and interested writers need to go no further than these volumes for research information of Bermuda's earliest written history.

Bermuda is a sub-tropical island in the Atlantic which lies over 700 miles southeast of North Carolina and northeast of Florida. It is known as the 'Emerald of the Sea,' because of its magnificent beauty. The shorelines of pink, sandy beaches retreat into a mixture of rich, green trees. The narrow, winding roads are lined with Oleander trees. When in bloom, they are full of pink and white flowers. Many trail ways have beautiful Poinciana trees which hang over the path. Flowers grow year-round in the warm climate. My grandfather was a Grower, with a lily field near his house. At harvest time, he sold the flowers to merchants throughout the island.

The homes in Bermuda now are built of cement block and painted in pastel colors. They are surrounded by the beauty of Hibiscus trees; each tree, when in full bloom, has its own unique color. In the earlier days, houses were built of Bermuda Limestone. It was hand-cut directly out of stone- quarries. Today, the limestone is only used for slating roof tops, which are then coated with white limestone wash. As you fly into the island, the roof tops are so white they look as though it had recently snowed. Rain is caught in well- designed water traps. The water then flows into pipes which lead to storage tanks, built under the houses. It is piped through the houses in modern-day plumbing. Some hotels and business are serviced by their own water distillation plants. However, most are serviced by government facilities.

Beneath the sea surrounding Bermuda's shoreline are coral reefs and tropical fish displaying magnificent colors. I've always reflected to myself, if fashion designers ever went snorkeling or diving around the coral reefs of Bermuda, they would be fascinated. You can see pictures of tropical fish in magazines, but you cannot see the incredible color changes as they disguise themselves for protection or ambushing prey. During this maneuver, the fish blend themselves within the coral.

With all the beauty surrounding the island, there was also a mystery. The island was known to many sea captains as the 'Devil's Isle,' because many vessels had shipwrecked on the unseen coral reefs. The following is an account of a shipwreck which was recorded in the manuscripts of Bermuda's history.

Approximately 150 adventurers, men, women and children, sailed on the Sea Venture, June 2, 1609, from England. Their intended destination was Jamestown, Virginia. After many days at sea, they encountered a storm. It lasted for four days.

In the darkness of the night, when no lamp could be kept alight because of the wind and spray, they expected every plunge of the groaning ship would be their last. They could only pray to inspire themselves and others with hope. In the morning, the brave souls stumbled out on deck to see the raging sea, a sight no one would ever forget. The waves covered the deck with white, boiling foam that seemed higher than the masts. The roar of the ocean was truly frightening. The laboring ship mounted a tremendous wave and then went down, as if to be swallowed by the angry sea, but she rose again on another wave and then sank to rise again and again. The storm was very powerful and continued for a few more days. On the fourth morning, there was stillness...One can recall the Bible story of Jesus calming the sea. Only He, our Almighty, powerful God, can make these waves and keep them within their bounds; only He can prevent their weak vessel from being dashed to pieces, and, if He chooses, He can say at any given moment, "*Peace, be still*," and, the sea would be calm.

Admiral Sir George Somers, when none of them had dreamed of such happiness, cried, "Land...land!" An unexpected coast had appeared. The ship had filled with water and was sinking. The Admiral drove the sinking ship onto the rocks and was able to transport the passengers safely to shore. All 150 men, women and children survived.

Some of these settlers remained on the island with their families. Others continued, later that year, with their voyage to Jamestown, Virginia. They had built a new ship from cedar trees found growing on the island.

Many sea captains did not know how to navigate the narrow coral reef channels that surrounded Bermuda, especially in the early days. In the middle of the deep Atlantic Ocean, one would not expect a reef. It seemed like a monster had grabbed the bottom of the boat and trapped it between its massive jaws. They soon realized that they had shipwrecked. Some of these ships have been traced back to their origins and dated back 400 years.

In later years, other ships got the aid of skilled St. David's sea pilots. My grandfather, Harry Granville Fox, was one. He and his small crew tried to be among the first to reach the ships appearing on the horizon. He and his crews made a living by piloting the ships into the harbor. They were paid by the captain. Today, with all the modern technology that ships have, they still have sea pilots who are now employed by the Government of Bermuda to provide this service.

Can you imagine what it is to cross an ocean? For weeks you see nothing but the horizon. Perfect and empty. You live in the grip of fear: fear of storms, fear of sickness, and fear of immensity. But, you must drive that fear down deep into your belly. Study your charts. Watch your compass. Pray for a fair wind and hope, pure naked, fragile hope. At first there's no more than a haze on the horizon, so you watch...you watch...then there's a smutch of shadow in the salt water. For a day after a day and another a day, the stain slowly spreads over the horizon taking form…until on the fourth day you let yourself believe; you dare to whisper the words, "Land…land…life…resurrection." You stand there amazed, the true adventure before your eyes, coming out of the vast unknown, out of the immensity into new life.

In the beginning of this journey, the ocean had given an image of eternity. The explorers must have asked themselves, "Did we discover this New World, or did the New World discover us?"

I have tried to imagine the early days of sea adventurers, when they did not have skilled sea pilots like my grandfather. Imagine, yourself, how frightening these shipwrecks must have been. In the middle of the Atlantic, caught in a raging storm, with hurricane winds, thunder and lightning, this had to be a horrifying event. The ship tossed from side to side, men scrambling for their lives, then suddenly, a loud crash! The ship was broken into pieces, and the men were tossed into the dark sea.

The next morning, I envision the calm after the storm, the stillness and fresh smell of salty air as the sun was beginning a new day; everyone who had survived was awakened by the rolling tide planting its kiss on the shore then rolling back out to sea, as if to say, "You're safe now! They found themselves thrust upon the most beautiful beach they had ever envisioned.

I imagine also the ocean as I've seen it many times in my lifetime, walking on the beaches from a young boy to a grown man; after a raging storm, the ocean becomes as smooth as glass. The sea is so clear that you feel as though you could drink it, so clear that you can see the bottom, so clear that you can see blue, gold, green and red-colored Parrot fish feeding on the coral next to you. I imagine how the shipwrecked travelers must have felt as they looked up from the beach and saw a forest of rich, green cedar trees which became the treasured pieces of furniture in their homes and also were used for the new ships they built. In my mind, I can hear the voices of The Admiral and his crew as they prayed, "Lord, thank You for sparing our lives, and thank You for giving us an island of paradise."

After beginning this story, several years ago, the phrase *Island of Paradise* became the title of my album, filled with the love of the home where I was born and the romantic life I had lived there.

> *"This island of mine, I'll love it 'till the end of time.*
> *Sweet memories of yesterday as love crossed my way."*

The treasures of my life are hidden in the words of the songs I have recorded. The CD entitled *Something Special* includes original songs written by me. I wish I could sing the words of my songs inspired by my life on the Island from the pages of this book, but I can't. So, just imagine yourself, for a moment, on the beautiful island of Bermuda and that you are sharing it with the perfect partner.

RESCUE AT SEA

The youngest son of my grandfather, my Uncle Ivan, also known as 'Conquer' or Captain Ivan Fox, lived in Larchmont, New York. He sailed through many storms on trips from Newport, Rhode Island to Bermuda as captain on board yachts visiting and returning to the United States.

Since Bermuda was situated in the middle of the Atlantic Ocean, it became a requirement for the young men of the island to master the sea. It was for their safety. Those who accomplished this became fishermen and sea pilots. Their training involved going out to sea at night to study the stars and learn how to navigate by first-hand experience. During the day, they would be taken out to sea where they could no longer see land and be trained to navigate back to the island.

This training became useful in many ways; when yacht owners sailed to Bermuda in the summer months, they added additional crewmen. On many occasions, the original crewmen would fly back to the United States. The yacht owners then recruited a new crew of islanders to assist them in the long voyage home. It became a way of life for my Uncle Ivan and many other young St. David's sea-farers. For my Uncle Ivan, the sea was like no other place he would want to be.

I remember many years ago in the summer he was on a yacht called the 'Wal-Dor' sailing from Newport, Rhode Island to

Bermuda. The yacht was owned by a retired, elderly man named Bill Schnirring from Larchmont, New York. He was accompanied on board by his wife and daughter, Susie. They were midway across the Atlantic when they got caught in a storm. The voyage brought world attention, as the news covered the rescue at sea. It was described as miraculous. As the storm tossed the yacht in the heavy seas, fortunately, my Uncle Ivan was able to send an SOS signal. A passing vessel responded to the rescue. The large vessel had to bridge ropes from their ship to the yacht. After accomplishing this maneuver, they were able to hoist Mr. and Mrs. Schnirring and their daughter, Susie, from the yacht up to the ship. My Uncle Ivan wanted to remain on the yacht to try to save it, but the seas were too heavy. Ivan was the last to be hoisted to the rescuing ship. The rescue ship's crew then tried to save the yacht, but it was impossible. As the boat was pulled through the heavy seas, it took in too much water. It began to sink, so it was finally cut loose.

Meanwhile, Susie knew her own daughter, Samantha, was safe but waiting through that terrible ordeal, not knowing what was happening at sea. The child was only four or five at the time. She had been flown to Bermuda by air earlier and was already safe in the arms of my grandmother. Susie had wanted Samantha to come on vacation to Bermuda with the family, but as a loving parent, had not wanted to have her travel by sea. The news reporters followed the story of the rescue right to my grandmother's home in St. David's. Samantha's photo in the arms of my grandmother, along with photos of the rescue, was on the front page of the Bermuda Royal Gazette.

My fondest memory of the 'Wal-Dor' was sailing off the east coast of Florida. My Uncle Ivan let me sail the yacht up to Savannah, Georgia. We sailed through the inter-coastal water way, and finally, out to sea through the channel at Fort Pierce. Exiting the mouth of Fort Pierce, the seas were rolling in very high, 10 to 20 foot swells. Later, I could imagine what it must have been like during the terrible storm in which this lovely yacht was lost.

As I mentioned in the beginning of this story, St. David's Islanders were men of the sea. My Uncle Ivan must have had to use every ounce of knowledge my grandfather taught him about how to sail the sea, and it became a way of life for him. He never stopped sailing after that day. Mr. Schnirring purchased another yacht, and my Uncle Ivan continued to be captain. They sailed until they both passed away of old sea-farers age.

My grandfather was not only a sea pilot on the island of Bermuda Shores, but he also travelled to England by sea to fight in the Second World War. He enjoyed sitting on the outside step of our old homestead house and telling stories to us kids, stories of the days when he was a sea pilot and fighting for Britain. His most painful memory was losing his best friend who was next to him in a foxhole during a battle. He always rejoiced in guiding the tall ships into the narrow channels and through the hidden coral reefs. He brought in ninety-nine vessels safely.

My mother's name is Illyria Fox; my grandfather named her after the Spanish tall ship "Illyria". He once guided this tall ship through the narrow channels of Bermuda.

ST. DAVID'S

Although there were many progressive developments throughout Bermuda, the focus of my story is about St. David's, where I was raised, its development and my personal journey.

On the 18th of November, 1940 the Governor announced to the people of Bermuda that half of St. David's would be leased to the United States Air Force Base for defense purposes. The American military soon arrived and built a base on the island of St. David's in preparation for the Second World War. The United States Air Force ground crew land-filled many shallow-water areas around St. David's and Castle Harbor and built an airport. Bermuda is so centrally located in the world that the United States later set up a tracking station on the island for their space program. On September 18, 1947, the United States Air Force became a separate agency under the newly-formed Department of Defense.

Although Bermuda had become a refueling and rest location during the last months of the Second World War, many visitors arrived in Bermuda by ship and by air. Tourism soon became a major part of Bermuda's economy and growth. Bermuda was not only able to prosper, it was able to support itself financially and not be totally dependent on the British Crown. However, today, Bermuda remains a dependent Colony of the British Commonwealth.

Bermudians, because of their prosperity over the years, have been able to travel, quite often internationally. They become educated, speak very well and are much in tune with what is happening in the world because of advanced telecommunications.

When the Air Force Base was established, St. David's was divided fairly much down the middle by a seven foot fence. The residents of St. David's were on one side and the military personnel were on the other side. However, jobs were available for many local residents.

The American servicemen brought many different cultures to the island of Bermuda and especially to St. David's islanders. The islanders began to mingle and integrate with military personnel, on many levels. As the St. David's islanders began to interact with the influx of the military, many of the local women married American servicemen.

The British Garrison set up camp in 1948-1949, in a separate site at St. David's Battery. This was when my mother met my father, an Englishman serving in the British military. My mother told me wonderful stories of how and when my father and she met, and how each time together was a romantic experience.

Their romance started the day they met at a movie theater. She did not recall the name of the movie they were watching, she only remembered that they caught each other's eyes and began to stare. They soon introduced themselves, and they dated from that day on. In the tiny village of St. David's, for them, just to be there was like being on a honeymoon on a tropical island. They sailed around the harbor during the day and went for moonlight walks on a sandy beach at night. There were many little, secluded, uninhabited islands off the main island, and so they would sail to an island off shore and go snorkeling around the coral reefs. On other occasions, they attended local cricket matches and soccer games. It was a British Colony, and most of the sports originated from England. They also went to nightclub dances. Caribbean calypso music and fiery limbo dancers were very popular then. Sometimes, the entertainment was held outside near the beach. My mother would blush a little and say. "Well, we were very much in love, those days."

There were only two restaurants in St. David's at the time: The Black Horse Tavern and the Mount Area. The Mount Area was the only restaurant that had a bar and a night club all in one very large building. One side was the indoor night club, and the other side, which was much larger, had an outdoor night club which featured Caribbean music. The middle was a bar and take-out restaurant. They served fresh fish daily. It became the best fish sandwich place on the island. People came from all over the island to see the entertainment, but most came for Clarence Borden (the owner) and Dolly Pitcher's (the cook) famous fish sandwich and fish chowder. Shark hash was a specialty as well.

I remember, as a young boy, in late 50s and early 60s; they had limbo and belly dancers. The belly dancers rolled their stomachs and put swords down their throats. The swords looked very real to me, but I'm sure it was a magic trick. Some say it is the positioning of the sword. I was only eight or ten then, when I peeked through the windows to see the show. During the day, it was not uncommon for my young parents to just prepare a fruit basket and have a picnic on a hillside overlooking the ocean. Mother told me that she and my father watched the sail boats with their white sails gliding along the turquoise waters. She then smiled and said, "It was a wonderful sight to see, especially on a beautiful sunny day with a cool breeze coming off the ocean." She continued describing the day, "You could see the beautiful and graceful Bermuda Long-tails, flying in and out of the cliffs and soaring through the air." The Bermuda Long-tail is a white bird with black trimming on its wings, and a long needle-like tail. They are about as large as a pigeon. In the winter months, the Long-tails fly further south. In the warmer summer months, they return to the Bermuda shorelines. The Bermuda long-tail is found nesting in some of the cliffs around the island. Bermudians have come to rely on them as a sign of an early summer and the return of tourists. Tourists vacationing on the island eventually inherited the name 'Long-tail'. It was not a disgraceful nick-name, but complementary.

Many of the visitors to the island were very wealthy and stayed in the most expensive hotels. Formal evening dress was required for dining and entertainment.

Over the years things changed, and the dress code was eased a little. Bermuda is still very much a sophisticated island. It has maintained very high standards of dress. The visitors got their nickname "Long-tail" because of their return visits during the summer months, and their graceful respect of the high standards of the island.

After dating each other for quite some time, my father proposed marriage to my mother. My mother accepted, of course, and the announcement of the wedding was read in the church. However, 'the powers that be' stopped the actual wedding. The British authorities did not want a white English soldier to marry a darker native Bermudian girl, so my father was denied permission by his military superior officers.

When my mother and father's marriage was disallowed, my father was separated from my mother and had to leave Bermuda. He was relocated to Malaysia.

After that day, my mother never wanted to be with another man. Little did they know, or maybe they did know, that I had been conceived. When I was born, mother brought me up as a fatherless child. My mother had to be both parents in all aspects of life.

Jay Fox, age 11, 1960 first in his class, St. David's Elementary..."He is doing so well; he has taken on new life in his class work."

– Cyril Butterfield. Teacher

WRITING

My interest in writing began in elementary school, the year I became first in my class. The teacher, Rev. C. Butterfield, was a part-time preacher and a full time teacher. He presented me with an adventure book titled, The Walton Boys. I found the story of their adventures to be very exciting. I began to see myself in those adventure stories and wrote about what I had imagined. My story, as one would read, seemed so real, but yet, it was only in my imagination.

After elementary, I attended St. George's Secondary School, a Government-controlled public school equivalent to a High School. I passed all the general subjects with satisfactory to excellent grades. I'll always remember the unforgettable year when President John F. Kennedy was assassinated on November 22nd, 1963. My class sat there in total shock at the news.

During my high school years, my mother and I lived on the base, because she worked as a live-in nanny for a Colonel of the U. S. Air Force. His wife had a serious illness which limited her activities. They had a little girl and young boy.

THE BIG PRESENT

On October 26, 1964, I celebrated my fifteenth birthday. It was an exciting year, as it was the beginning of my entertainment career. A few days earlier, I had headed to Hamilton, the capital city of Bermuda. In the city were many stores of all sorts; however, I was headed for one in particular, a music store.

I grew up as a young boy watching the *'Ozzie and Harriet Show,'* a family program with two young boys, David and Ricky Nelson. The star of the show, to me, was none other than their son, Ricky. He had the admiration of probably every young man, because we learned from him how to attract the girls. I watched as Ricky played the guitar at teen dances, and the girls went wild with excitement. He was a young entertainer in the early 60's and 70's, like Elvis Presley. He also starred in several old western movies with the most famous cowboy, John Wayne.

Ricky inspired me to play guitar, as well. While in the music shop in the city of Hamilton, I saw an ordinary acoustic guitar. As I plucked on the strings, I thought that this would be a fine guitar to start with. I returned home that evening to hint the news to my mom of what I'd like for a birthday gift. At the dining room table I just busted out, "Mom, I'd love to have a guitar for my birthday; there's a very inexpensive acoustic guitar at the 'Music Box' in Hamilton!" I continued my 'persuasion' and explanation by saying, "I would love to learn how to play like Ricky Nelson;

he's so popular and sings at teen dances." For a moment, my Mom just sat there and listened. I was not sure whether she agreed or disagreed about purchasing the guitar.

The birthday came, and sure enough, I opened the BIG present. To my surprise it really was a guitar, but listen to this; it was not the guitar I had wished for. With absolute delight and excitement, I saw that the guitar in the box was a Candy Apple Red electric guitar with chrome trim. I had never dreamed of getting anything this wonderful.

The most incredible birthday gift I've ever received was my first guitar; it took me to places I would have never dreamed.

Thanks Mom.

I suppose any young man whose parent was not wealthy would be as surprised as I was. Immediately, I said, "Mom, this guitar must have been expensive; I did not expect this one." I probably did not see it in the music shop at the time because my mind was focusing on something that we could afford. My Mother told me that she had spent a little extra on a better and more attractive guitar, so I would stick with it and really learn to play it. That, I did. I taught myself, through music books and by ear, how to play the guitar.

At the beginning, it was easier to make up my own songs than it was to learn a song from the radio. This is when I began writing original songs. The songs were compilations of day to day life's experiences. As I started playing these songs for my friends, I began by telling the stories about what inspired the songs before singing them for others. Later, when I told the stories and performed these songs professionally, the audience always commented favorably, and left intrigued. This became my trademark as a performer. It was a thrill to fascinate the audience; as they say, "I had the audience in the palm of my hands." The joy was immediate gratification. The guitar had become a best friend, and only a musician can understand that phrase.

Within a year after my fifteenth birthday, I got together with an American friend, named Bob Johnson. He played the drums; my best friend, Llewellyn Hall, played the bass, and my cousin, Edmund Fox, played lead guitar. I added the rhythm guitar and was leader and manager of the group. A young pop band was born. The very first band we started was called The *Bi-ington Whistle*. Edmund came up with the name. Don't ask him what inspired the name; he just said it was the first thought on his mind. I and the other members of the band were puzzled, but we liked the name. It kind of grew on you.

The **Biington** *Whistle*
Jay Fox, Bob Johnson, Llewelyn Hall and Edmund Fox

We soon started learning songs and playing at functions and teen dances. It was lots of fun playing some of Ricky Nelson's songs and many others in that era. The most popular songs we played were songs of the *Beatles* and the *Rolling Stones*.

Our first performance was at a beach BBQ at Clear Water Beach on Kindley Air Force Base. It was for the enlisted men of the U. S. military. While playing for the men in the military, we met an excellent guitarist named Greg Whitman. He once played in a band with Jim Web. Jim wrote many songs over the years. The *5th Dimension* and Glen Campbell recorded a few of his songs. Greg soon joined the group and added the Californian music of the *Beach Boys*. Greg could sure play the guitar; he was one of the best I've ever heard. He was up there with Jimmy Hendrix and Eric Clapton. I learned a lot from him.

I'll never forget our biggest appearance. It was July 4th, as thousands of people attended to see the 'Blue Angels' fly over and perform their aerial show at Kindley Field. We performed on a flatbed trailer. That day, we were exposed to the notice of several club managers from around the island. After that performance, we received many bookings.

Edmund, after a few years in the band, went on to a college in England. Soon after, Bob, a United States Air Force officer's son, returned to the United States with his family. Greg, also, was transferred to another base. At this time, Llewelyn quit the band as well.

During this time, my life, outside entertainment, was busy. I graduated from St. George's Secondary School at the age of sixteen in 1965. I did not go to college. In 1966, I began working at the Kindley Air Force Base commissary. After a few years, I received a Superior Performance Award for outstanding work from Horace A. Stevenson, JR. Colonel, U.S.A.F. Commander.

I continued my interest in music, started my second band and named it *The Variations*. I added a drummer named Earl Wescom.

I played guitar and found a lead singer named David Faries. We, later, gave him the nick-name 'Little Dave.' He only stood about 5 foot 7 inches, making him the shortest member of the group, but, he had a big voice. His brother George joined us as a back-up vocalist. We had a vocal harmony similar to the *Bee Gees*.

We performed at the Gun Powder Tavern in St. George's one summer. It is an historic gun powder storage bunker used many years ago for the British military, long before United States became independent from England. Many years later, it was converted into a tavern.

The Variations became very popular throughout the island of Bermuda, performing on weekends at local clubs and high school teen dances. It was at one of the early teen dances that I met my first steady girl friend. She was fifteen, about to turn sixteen; I was seventeen and about to turn eighteen. As teenagers, we had an incredible adventure of our own. Our young romance was short lived, but, our meetings after many years of absence were extraordinary. Enjoy the following true love story.

THE SACRED COVE

One day, I sat looking at my first love's high school photo. Her name is Donna. She was sixteen in the photo; I was a little older. Taking a high school photo is so nerve-racking; you're just sitting there looking directly into the camera. It's like taking a driver's license photo. The person being photographed never likes the results. What I remember is the real person, that incredible young girl, a bit shy, but she had a wonderful smile. Singing the song 'Oh, Donna' brought that smile out.

I had started my second band, *The Variations*, at the time, and we were performing at a teen dance. Donna looked like she was tickled to death as she stood next to the stage to hear me play my guitar and sing. We met after the dance and dated for quite some time after that. I never knew that she had a confidence problem or lack of strength until she told me.

My fondest memories were the moments we sat on the back stairs of her home. We'd kiss, and I'd nibble on her ear. It seemed she was about to climb walls. Speaking of climbing walls, I had to climb over the wall just to get to her. Her house was surrounded by high walls, like most celebrities; however, her dad was not a celebrity. He was a military official. The extra effort to see her was worth it though.

One night, she had to baby-sit a few miles from her home. I came over, and we had such a great time. We heard a car coming in the driveway. Her sister came running into the house to tell her that her mother was coming. Donna had told her sister that she had a date over. Her mother must have heard that conversation and came to investigate.

When her mother arrived, in panic, I had to jump out of the back window. Little did I know, the drop was fifteen to twenty feet! The fall could have broken my leg. I loved her so much that I would have jumped from a two-story building, not to get her in trouble.

We laughed so much, the next day after recalling that incident. I reminded her that her sister had saved us from misery, that night. Misery came much later when she ran away from home. We were so young and so much in love. I think our parents were afraid that we wanted to get married. I don't know what made her leave home; maybe it was the lack of confidence and strength she had talked about. When she left home, she came straight to me. I was going to take her back home, immediately, but we both knew we were going to be punished, so we rode my motor bike to a secluded beach and spent the night in a sandy cove. It frightens me to death when I think of it today. What if the tide had risen high that night? Surely, God protected us. I now call it "The Sacred Cove."

The next day was a sunny morning. It was beautiful to see the sunrise on her face. We swam in the ocean for a while and spent a wonderful day together. As the evening drew near, I rode my motor bike along south shore of the island with her sitting on the back, holding me tightly around my waist. We were headed to who knows where. We ended up several miles from where we started, and sat on a hillside overlooking the ocean. We watched the sun set as it glowed on the calm, mirror-like sea. As the sun slowly entered the water, it was as though a gold coin had been inserted into a melting pot; it created an incredible sunset glow and golden pathway from where we were sitting. It looked as though the path was leading into a magical, mystery journey. The colors reflected into the evening sky, as the stars began to come out and twinkle, one by one. Can you picture in your mind for a moment what that was like? It was so romantic and peaceful. We sat there for hours.

Reality hit us when we realized we could not stay lost forever. We got back on my motor bike and headed home to face the consequences of staying out all night. We were separated after that day and never saw each other again for many years.

The Variations
David 'Little Dave' Faries, Earl Wescom, George Faries and Jay Fox
The Gun Power Tavern in St. Georges, 1970.

The Variations
Jay Fox, Leroy Jones, Hiram Edwards and *Llewellyn Hall;*
David Faries 'Little Dave is seated.

THE VARIATIONS

The band went through many changes in personnel in the beginning years, but I was determined to keep a band going.

When I was about 21-22 the group changed again. It was made up of me on guitar, Llewellyn rejoined on bass and Leroy Jones played drums. Our star attraction was 'Little Dave.' He became popular singing *The Beatles, Rolling Stones, Bee Gees* and *Neil Diamond*. Later, his interest began to lean toward the style of *Tony Orlando* who had the big hit, *Tie a Yellow Ribbon*. He was very popular then and had a hit TV Show. 'Little Dave' looked like Tony and sang like him, and girls went crazy over him.

As his popularity grew, his interest in the style of his music changed. The group changed our style of music from a dance band to a Show Band and added a trumpet player named Hiram Edwards. It was at this time that Little Dave began singing *Tom Jones* songs from his popular TV show. The group performed in the hotel circuit for a few years, but our taste in music began to change once again. Llewellyn and Hiram quit the group and went in different directions. They wanted to form a Big Band sound. They were both very talented musicians. Rock & Roll was easier to play for the rest of the band. It was less complicated.

In 1971, I was now 22. The Holiday Inn had built a large hotel in the old town of St. George's; I resigned from the Air Force base commissary and began a new career in the new hotel. Although I began working in the hotel during the day I continued my interest in music.

Bermuda was very strict with their immigration laws so I had to advertise in the local paper for new musicians. I wanted musicians who played a variety of music to appeal to the enlisted men and women of the U.S. military.

Many of the United States military troops were returning home from Vietnam and were stationed at the base for a year before continuing to the U.S. If you have seen the movie *Forest Gump,* starring Tom Hanks, the music in the movie was from that era. I wanted my band to be part of helping the troops make a transition back to a normal life. Most of the local musicians who were good already had bands.

During the time that the band was developing I played a lot of basketball at the Base gym. At the gym, I met many great musicians who were in the United States Military. At the time, in 70's, the island was booming with local bands forming. It was the era when the Beatles were discovered. I was unable to find local musicians, so I hired excellent musicians from the United States Military. Some of the musicians that I was able to hire had played beside great bands as opening acts in the United States.

A keyboard player named Gene Stone from Macon, Georgia and a new bass player named Lynn Audrey from Texas joined the band. Leroy Jones continued playing drums in the band for a while longer. The two new members had been drafted into the U. S. military and were all stationed at the Base. Their duties were like a normal 8-5 job. They had time off nights and weekends.

The band continued to perform in the local clubs and at the Air Force and Naval bases as well as shows at the "Jungle Room." That was one of the hottest night spots in the city of Hamilton. The club featured exciting limbo acts, dancing on broken glass. Back stage, the band watched the dancers break beer bottles and spread the glass on a mat to dance on. We were the featured pop band and followed their act.

Bermuda Limbo Dancers at the *'Jungle Room'*

During this time when I was 22, Gene, Audrey, Jim Carlson and I rented a beautiful house in the middle of the island. Jim was not in the band; he was a good friend who served in the Navy with Gene and Audrey. The band had become very successful, and I felt that it was time to leave my mother's home in St David's. The four of us moved to a very large house located in Flatt's Village. We called it "Master View Palace," because of its magnificent view.

'Flatt's Village' this is an aerial view.

After our performances, we frequently met girls who had come to vacation during "College Week in Bermuda." It was a fabulous time on the island. We were living every young man's dream. Most of the college students arrived from the north-east coast of the United States and Canada.

The city of Hamilton buzzed with college students and local students combined. There were night spots on every block on Front Street, which was the main hub in the city for shops, late night restaurants and clubs. It was a great place to have fun and let loose for the summer holidays. Hamilton harbor was filled with cruise ships and boats of all sorts.

At night there was partying in every club. During the day, students hit the beach. The beaches were filled with college students all through the week. Our band only performed a few days during the week and most weekends. During our time off, we spent time having fun, socializing.

It was summer in Bermuda, and there were girls, girls, girls everywhere of all sorts and shapes. It was like being in the midst of a fruit platter with many sweet desserts to choose from. I'm sure the Bermudian island girls dated college guys from the East coast as well. It was a good time to be young and carefree.

In 1972, age 23, one particular night, I met a wonderful girl named Janet, and Gene was introduced to her best friend. After the show, we went dancing at a late-night disco. Later, we had breakfast at an all-night restaurant. We dropped the girls off later at the hotel where they were staying. The next day and during that week, Jan and I spent a lot of time together. It was daylight savings time, so after working at Holiday Inn during the day, it was still very warm and a perfect time to hit the beach. Evenings, we all got together and had cookouts at 'Master View Palace.'

It turned out to be a romantic vacation for Jan and me. I showed her most of the island by land and sea. She had a rented scooter, and I had my own motor bike to travel throughout the island. I left my car at home on beautiful days and nights. Motor bikes were the best way to travel on the island. I had a Sea Ray speed boat as well as a small Sunfish sail boat. On land and water, we spent all our free time together. Jan and I began to try to build our relationship after that wonderful week. She was from Springfield, Massachusetts, in an area called Holyoke. I don't know how I got enchanted by a girl from a little town in another country, but one finally captured my heart. She had long, black silky hair and a smile that would capture any guy's heart, no matter how much of a 'player' he was.

After she returned home from her vacation, we communicated long-distance for quite some time. However, it was the distance between us that broke my heart. We could only see each other for a few weeks out of the year. I visited her in U.S., and she visited me on the island. It went on like this for two years. She did not want to give up her home, and I did not want to leave Bermuda. I could not leave the island life, because it was a part of me, and I was entwined with its culture. Being an entertainer, I had become a big part of what the vacationers came to see, as well as the sun, the beaches and the peacefulness of the island.

One cold, winter, long weekend when I was visiting Jan, Gene travelled with me to visit her friend. We arrived in Holyoke and stayed at her parent's home. It was late that evening, when we met with her parents, sister and friends, then later, had dinner. After getting acquainted, the night was soon over. The next evening, Jan planned a wonderful dinner for the four of us. The meal was great, and after dinner, the setting could not have been better for a perfect evening, with a glass of wine, sitting in front of the fireplace. It was cold and snowing outside, so I, good ole Jay, a Bermudian from sun and beaches, decided to start a fire. The fireplace was going great, but I forgot to open the vent. Of course, you know what happened. If you're not from the cold, wintery north, you probably would not know all the procedures you should do any more than I did. When one lights a fire, one should always open the air vent. This allows the smoke to be drawn up the chimney. Instead of a cozy scene, the living room became quickly filled with smoke.

Everyone else who was still finishing up in the dining room scrambled into the living room thinking the house was on fire. Gene corrected that problem very quickly, and the evening turned out great after all.

The next day, we headed to Brody Mountain to the ski slopes. Gene and I did not know how, being from the south and from an island. We had never snow-skied before. Jan began to teach me, and Gene's date began to teach him. We had a great day, even if I came down the slopes sideways and sometimes backwards. I finally got the hang of it. Actually, within a few hours, I learned how to ski. I had water-skied often and the balancing on snow skis was similar. After skiing all day, we decided to stay at the ski club for the entertainment that night. We continued to have a great time until it was time to leave.

By this time, fog and snow had been getting thicker all evening. When we headed down the mountain, we barely could see two feet in front of us. We drove very slowly, and nearly at the bottom, we ran out of gas. Jan and I were elected to fetch gas in the darkness. As she and I walked through the snow, the drift felt like it was two feet high. We finally got to a house, and the lights were still on. I began to get frightened and thought maybe someone would come out and shoot us for trespassing. We finally made it to the door. It had a small window, so one could see who was there from the inside. I rang the door bell; within a minute a face suddenly appeared. Looking at the face in the small window, I said, "Oh no, Jan. We're in for it." The door slowly opened, and a man stood at the entrance. "No gun, thank God!" was my first thought. We told him why we were there and asked if he could help us. He did, and was very kind and understanding. He must have had that situation happen before even if I never had.

Our time ran out, and Gene and I headed back to Bermuda. He had to get back to his military duties, and I had to get back to my hotel job. Playing in the band was just a part-time job for us.

THE BERMUDA REGIMENT

When I was twenty two, I was drafted into the Bermuda Regiment. We had to serve for three years; however, it was not full-time. We were still able to continue our regular jobs. We only had to go for duty once or twice a week and on training trips to Jamaica. We also trained for military combat, but most of our time was spent clearing damage after hurricanes. Other times, we were in parades. The Regiment was part of the military security for the visits of Presidents from other countries. The Bermuda Regiment Honor Guard and several other marching units formed up for the Queen's Birthday Parade and other Government ceremonies each year.

Jay Fox

I had many memorable experiences in the Bermuda Regiment. My most interesting time was when His Excellency the Governor, Sir Richard Christopher Sharples and his Aide-de-Camp Captain Hugh Ralph Lorne Sayers were both assassinated, March 10th, 1973. When he was assassinated, one of my duties was to search Government grounds with my platoon from the Bermuda Regiment. We had to find any clues as to who had shot the governor. My platoon, along with many other police officers and investigators, stretched across the full length of the 40 acres. I am certain we searched every square inch. We set up headquarters on the property and sent out patrols daily and every night until the investigations were completed.

One night, when it was very dark, I sent out my patrol. Two soldiers from the platoon were to circle the Government House. As the men patrolled the grounds, they passed by a very tall hibiscus hedge. Behind the hedge, they heard a rustling sound.

The two soldiers called headquarters where I was in command. I immediately assembled a few troops, with their rifles, to investigate. As we searched behind the hedge, rifles cocked and ready for anyone who might jump out in front of us, the rustling sound became louder. Finally, we discovered the culprit; it was a vegetable garden being soaked with water. A Government House gardener had left the garden sprinkler on. It had a circular motion, and the sound of the water coming out of the hose hitting the dry leaves every few seconds sounded to the patrol guards like someone was lurking in the bushes. After reassuring my troops that the sprinkler was harmless, I instructed them to disarm and head back to headquarters. I then called into Government House, told them what had happened and requested them to have someone shut off the garden hose, coming out from under the door of a locked shed. It had caused so much excitement, and now the guys were alert to any suspicious movement.

'Government House'

At that time, there were also police officers on duty inside Government House. After all the commotion was settled, the patrol guards were ordered to continue, around the building. The evening got darker; all was very quiet and still. Every little cricket or tree-frog sounded, to the guards, louder than usual. The men heard a crunching sound behind them; already disturbed by the water hose incident, they were very alert. When they had passed by the front door of the Government House, a police officer on duty inside had decided to come out for a cigarette break. Instead of coming out in front of the patrol guards, so he could be visible, he came out after they had passed the door. At that moment, they immediately turned, leveled their rifles and yelled, "Halt." The officer stood there in total shock, eyes opened wide, mouth slack as the cigarette dropped to the ground. His pants were wet. He was absolutely shaken, as the guards and another officer told me later.

The police officer had made the foolish mistake coming out of the building behind the guards, and could have been killed. The poor guy; a cigarette break for him almost turned into a nightmare. He would never forget that moment, I'm sure. Luckily, the troops were trained to turn and look first, before confrontation. After the incident was reported to me, I changed the patrol guards before they shot someone accidently.

While I was stationed at Government House, I was still dating Jan; she had become very fond of Bermuda. When she heard of the assassination, she was horrified. She sent a telegram from Holyoke to a local flower shop in Bermuda and arranged for me to pick up flowers. She asked me to deliver them to the Governor's wife as a gesture of condolence for her loss. Since I was there with the Regiment during the investigations, I figured this was no problem, so I delivered them. Can you believe that the investigating officers called me into their office and questioned why I had delivered flowers? I was in military uniform, so you can imagine I was stunned at the gesture. Thank God, they later told me it was just procedure. We were all on edge because of the assassination.

Later, during the funeral of the Governor, I had the honor of carrying his sword during the procession. There were thousands of onlookers on both sides of the street as I marched down the middle. I was ahead of the rest of the procession. I also had the honor of boarding the war ship which carried the funeral procession from the city of Hamilton and along the northern ocean shore line to the old town of St. George's for his burial.

The Bermuda Regiment Honor Guard

While I was still in the Bermuda Regiment, my platoon was assigned to travel to Jamaica for training in their high mountains. Again, the same troops in my platoon were together. We packed our personal supplies and military equipment, and all headed to the airport. After boarding, the flight took off; it was very smooth. The flight took several hours. It was the longest trip by air most of us had ever made. After several hours in flight headed south toward the Caribbean islands, we were about to land, there was total silence; when the plane landed it felt like the wheels were about to explode. We all knew that it was fully loaded with army equipment and supplies. It was heavy. When it finally leveled out on the runway, all the troops shouted in jubilation; there were cheers from everyone on board. It was a scary moment, but we arrived safely.

We disembarked the airplane and entered the small airport. After collecting our personal baggage and equipment, we were given instructions to carry out the mission that we had been briefed on a few weeks earlier. Our mission was to travel over the hills and across a fast-flowing river on bamboo rafts.

The Bamboo Raft in Jamaica' Jay is on the left.

After several hours hiking, we came upon a small village. It was near the river bank. Women were standing in the water washing clothes. A few men were fishing, and several children were playing on the shore. That area had been cleared of all the bamboo stalks, and what was left was on the other side. We needed to make a raft in order to get the supplies across. We had to swim across the flowing river, first with a rope to bridge it from one side to the other. One of my men thought he was a strong swimmer and volunteered to make the first attempt. The current was so powerful; it swept him down the river a hundred yards or more. He almost drowned, but he managed to swim back to shore on the side he had started from. Two or three of the troops rushed down the river bank to see if he was okay. He was but was extremely shaken from the ordeal. In Bermuda we don't have fast-flowing rivers, and this was a new experience for him. A local Jamaican swimmer, who was watching us struggle to get across the river, came up to us and said, "Hey Mon, let me show you how to cross the water." Standing in front of the men with a bare chest and cut-off shorts, he looked like an expert in this maneuver. He took the rope, tied it to his waist and jumped into the river, swimming with the stream. He made it over to the other side in one attempt. On the other side, he tied the rope to the bamboo stalks. The men were now able to get across safely.

On the river bank, there were many tall bamboo stalks. We cut what we needed to build the raft. It took about a dozen stalks, sixteen feet long, tied together. Floating on the water, it could hold four men. Testing it out with this much weight, I knew, carrying two men, together weighing at least 350 lbs, it would be able to carry supplies that only weighed in, total, 200 lbs. It worked out just as planned. We then pulled everything across without incident. It took most of the morning to carry out this task. When all this was accomplished, we gave the used raft to the Jamaican swimmer who helped us. We began our journey through the rough terrain. Up ahead was a huge mountain. This took the rest of the day and into the evening; we set up tents and slept for the night.

The second day, after hiking half-way up the mountain, we were very hot. The platoon found a very large fresh water pond. We were making good time, so I allowed the men to take a break.

The next thing that I saw was the men stripping to take a quick swim. They had a great time diving off the rocks. That evening we settled on top of the mountain in the mist of clouds. My platoon once again built tents, sat around a camp fire and made dinner of cooked rice and corned beef. I must say, for camping, it was good.

In the evening, while the rest of the platoon were about to fall asleep, I summoned one of my best men. The soldier and I took a compass and a map of the island to plot out our direction for our next day's travel. The next morning arrived, and my platoon packed up once again and headed out for our destination, Port au Prince, a three to four day walk through the mountains.

We made it in good time with no serious incidents; however, we did pass a marijuana field. Along the border of the marijuana field, stood natives with machetes, as we passed through the area, my men and the natives just glared at each other; nothing was said. Those few moments were very intense. We were not on a combat training trip. This was just a rough terrain experience. Our rifles were not loaded with ammunition, and we were not prepared for confrontation. Our mission was not tracking down drug dealers; although, it may have been part of an undisclosed mission with the higher-ranking Officers. Thankfully, the platoon arrived safely at the camp grounds in Port au Prince unharmed. The field was reported to the local authorities for them to deal with the situation.

At Port au Prince, the camp ground was spread out like a home-made village. There were tents everywhere you turned. Several platoons, officers and supplies were all now in one large area. My platoon was not due to arrive until the fourth day; however, we arrived early. I'll never forget the look on Captain Raynor's face when he saw me coming up the path with my troops. It was early in the morning, at day break. He was outside, washing his face in a make-shift basin. He looked up and was totally surprised. He said, "Corporal Fox, I was not expecting you and the platoon until tomorrow." Since we arrived early, we were awarded the following day off for leisure. The troops settled in and set up our own camp-site near the other platoon.

The next day was a day of leisure, while walking through the camp-ground I met up with the Sergeant Major, he was talking to a Jamaican Defense Force helicopter pilot. The Sergeant Major introduced me to him. The pilot and I hit it off very quickly. Maybe it was because of what I said.

"Sir, how do you like flying my helicopter."

Surprised, he replied, "What do you mean?"

I then pointed to the initials on the side of the helicopter JDF. I knew, and he knew, that it stood for the 'Jamaican Defense Force,' but, as a joke, I said, "JDF. Doesn't it mean 'Jay David Fox?'

To my surprise, he smiled and said, "Well, if it's yours, how would you like to go up for a ride?"

Excited about his invitation, I asked, "Are you serious?"

He said, "Yes!"

I replied, "Of course."

The Sergeant Major said, "Go, and enjoy the view from the sky."

I, bubbling with joy, was ready to experience a ride of a lifetime; I had never done this before. The pilot and I boarded the helicopter. He started the engine. The blades were spinning, and debris was flying about; the chopper lifted off. High in the sky, I looked out of the window of the chopper, and I could see the Sergeant Major on the ground. He now looked like a little plastic soldier like the kids play with. He was crossing his heart the way Catholic priests do. He knew he was responsible for me if anything happened. The flight and scenery from the air was fantastic. However, every turn or change of altitude, I could feel the movement. It felt as though I was riding a roller coaster. It was not like a normal airplane that was steady in flight. They usually fly above the clouds. In those flights you could not see anything.

In the helicopter, we flew over the mountain and through the canyon my platoon had hiked over the day before. From the air, it was a thick green forest. Flowing from the top of the mountain was a foamy, white waterfall that had created the rapid currents in the river below that we had to cross. We spent about 40 or so minutes flying over that area of the island. Below, the pilot pointed out Montego Bay with white sandy beaches. We then flew back to the camp grounds and landed safely. I, of course, thanked the Jamaican helicopter pilot and joked once again as he was leaving, "Be sure to take care of my chopper."

He looked back with a grin, and waved as he said, "Okay, Mon."

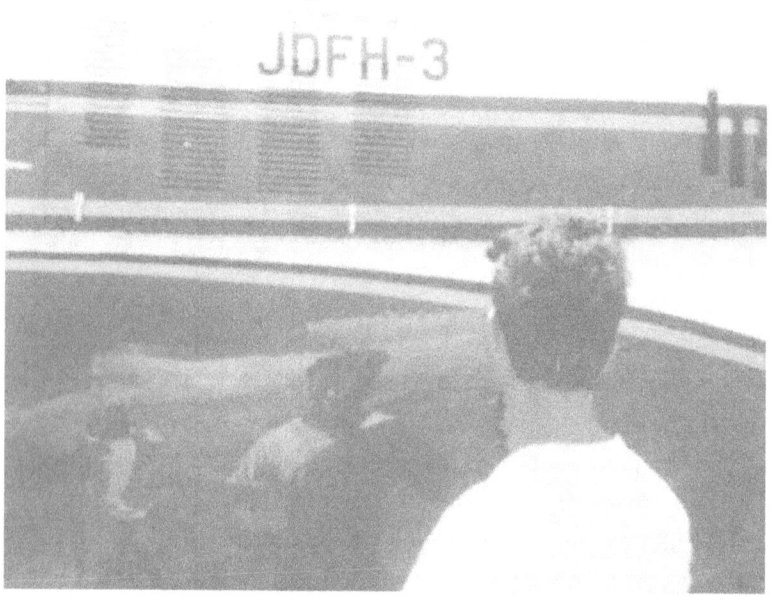

Later, I joined the rest of my platoon and told them of my experience. There was lots of envy, but my troops and I got along very well. After all, I had taken them on expeditions they had never been on and had brought them through without harm.

In the afternoon, a few of us traveled into the village and marketplace. The market place was bustling with tourists. There was a huge cruise ship along the dock. Children were diving off the dock for money. Noticeable in the crowd of shoppers, were children begging for money. In Bermuda you did not see much of this. It was rather sad. It showed the difference between the Bermuda Government and the Jamaican Government, and how prosperous our island had become compared to Jamaica.

After a few weeks, I finally returned to Bermuda from my regiment training in Jamaica. It was good to be back at 'Master View Palace'. The servicemen in the band told me about their summer. There was good news, and there was bad news. I'll start with the bad news. Jim Carlson, one of the guys who shared 'Master View Palace' with us, had a horrible motorcycle accident. His right arm was paralyzed. He could no longer ride his bike and was later discharged from the United States Navy. We had lost a great house buddy, but we were thankful that he survived the accident and that his injuries were not more serious.

Audrey, my bass player, had met a girl and had proposed to marry her. Gene had also met a girl and could not wait until I got home to meet her. When she left that evening, I told Gene that his single life was over. She was beautiful. I knew she would be the one he would soon marry.

We soon got right back into our band bookings. "College Week in Bermuda" was our busiest time of the year. It repeated each week throughout the summer vacations. One night, after the band had performed, we got home very late. Gene and I were still wide awake, so we sat on my water bed talking until we fell asleep. Water beds were popular then, so we had one in every room. The next morning I awakened with my show clothes still on and my acoustic guitar beside me. I still had my guitar, because the last thing I remembered was working on a few lines for a new song. I often fiddled around with the guitar before drifting off to sleep. Gene added a few lines to the song, at times. Somehow, during the night as we were sleeping, I had pulled the plug out of the water mattress. The water was warm, so I had not noticed it. It was as if I were wrapped in a warm blanket. It did not over-flow unto the carpet, because the bed frame was lined with plastic.

However, the heated fluid had leaked out to fill the frame box, and I awakened, soaking wet. I immediately floundered out and began to shout, "I'm wet! I'm wet!" as I dripped on the carpet, startling Gene awake. "I've got to change and go to work." I still worked at Holiday Inn during the day and had to go to work that morning. It was the weekend, and fortunately, I only needed to go in for a few hours to finish a project. Gene had the weekend off, so he got stuck remaining home to fix the water bed problem.

Gene had invited Lynn, the college girl he had just met, over to go sailing that afternoon. I was to join them after work. We had an incredible, fun time the rest of the day. We went sailing in St. George's harbor. The afternoon was beautiful, slightly windy, a perfect breeze for a small Sunfish sailing boat. Gene and I were teaching Lynn how to sail. After a few hours, the wind picked up, very strong. Lynn got confused as to whether she had to pull the sail in or let it out to balance the boat. In her confusion, she pulled the sail in too tight. If you know anything about a Sunfish sail boat, this was a "no, no." Within a second, the strong wind had tipped over the boat. The three of us were thrown overboard. We were now hanging on to the side of the overturned boat. The wind was so strong, at this point, that it was difficult to upright the boat again. However, we did not panic. We just hung on and began laughing like crazy at our second water adventure of the day.

We did not realize that we were drifting along, now, in very choppy waters, about a mile off shore in the harbor. Things were beginning to get serious. Thankfully, there were many houses along the shoreline. A family was sitting out on their lawn chairs, enjoying the day. They observed the whole situation. They soon realized we were in real trouble. They immediately got into their Boston Whaler boat to come out and rescue us. It was a small, outboard, motorized boat which could seat about six to eight people. Within minutes, we were picked up. The sailboat was towed to a dock near their home. The kind folks who rescued us provided us with large towels to keep us from shivering. We were thankful. After awhile, they drove Gene and Lynn back to my car. I, then, sailed the Sunfish back to its mooring where Gene picked me up.

Our group continued to do a show every weekend throughout the year at the 'Jungle Room' in the city of Hamilton. Although we did shows during college weeks throughout the summer, we continued to be a dance band the rest of the year. Our lead singer, 'Little Dave's,' interest began to grow more into the show-cabaret style. Later, he quit *The Variations* and joined an all-brass show band. Leroy, the drummer, married my cousin Gerry, got an offer to play nightly in a jazz band in the hotel circuit and accepted. I continued the excitement of a dance band, performing the hits of the 70's. I kept the name *The Variations*, and added new musicians. What an exciting sound we produced. I'm glad I decided to continue to call us *The Variations*, because Bermuda is a multicultural island and enjoyed many different types of music.

After a few more years, the servicemen who had been in my group were discharged from the military. Gene returned to Macon, Georgia. He did, eventually, marry Lynn, and they had four children. Gene and I had become very close, like brothers. He said, when he got married, he would name his son after me. Well, the day came. When Lynn and he were about to have their first child, he called me on the phone back in Bermuda. I had to prepare him, so I said, "Gene, what if it is a girl?" He said, "I'll name her, Jessica." Sure enough, it was a girl. They tried again a few years later, and guess what? Lynn, had triplets; two girls and a boy. Gene and Lynn were in a state of shock. It made the local news in his little town. Since he used the "J" for Jessica, they named the triplets, Megan, Morgan and Matthew. He never did name a child after me, but I was flattered that he would want to. He and Lynn quit after four children.

Jan and I eventually broke up; the long-distance relationship and loneliness in between visits were driving me crazy. It was at Audrey's wedding that Jan and I felt that it was time to move on. Audrey's wedding was held in Massachusetts. The band was in the wedding party. A few days after the wedding, Jan and I talked about our situation and decided that we should just remain as friends. Our friendship continued for awhile, but as time over the years passed, we no longer had contact. When *The Variations* disbanded after that great summer of 1973, I had no desire to start another band. It was so difficult putting together a good one, so I pursued my hotel career, fulltime. I no longer needed 'Master View Palace' living alone, so I returned to St. David's to live. It was closer to the Holiday Inn.

CAREER AND MARRIAGE

When I had first joined the Holiday Inn in 1971 at age 22, I was very upfront with the Controller. He was responsible for hiring new staff. I was very bold and explained to him that I would give a 100% in all that I do if I was hired; however, my first love was being an entertainer, which required a 110%, and I would need a flexible schedule. I was hired. He then told me to enroll in Hotel Management courses. I embraced his advice, and enrolled in correspondence courses from The Educational Institute of The American Hotel and Motel Association, Lansing, MI. The final exams were arranged at the Bermuda College. I received certificates in many areas. They were gold stamped for distinction in Food and Beverage Management, F&B Controls, F&B Purchasing, Human Resource, Supervisory and Training Skills.

At the beginning of my hotel career, I started out as a stock handler. I was, eventually, promoted to Head Store Man. I then was promoted to Receiver in control of every supply entering the hotel. I passed up further promotions because of the band. After the band disbanded and I could concentrate all my energy on my job, I accepted a promotion to Food and Beverage Controller.

Within only a few years, I had a streak of promotions. Each time I was promoted, I taught and trained another young person willing to advance his or her career. They, eventually, were promoted to take my previous position. Holiday Inn was a brand-new luxury hotel, and joining an enterprise at the beginning had its advantages. There were several fine restaurants in the hotel from which to choose; cuisines ranged from native to French to fast-food. My responsibility as a Food and Beverage Controller was to keep track of the cost of all food and beverage supplies entering the hotel and to keep inventory control. This included the cost to each outlet.

In addition to the several restaurants, there were night clubs and bars in the hotel and surrounding areas: beach, golf course, etc. I was required to cost every single item in each recipe on the menu and everything that was in each cocktail drink; the cost was then given a sales price. Each variety of cocktail served averaged a cost of 16%-18% of the sales price, and the food served averaged 32%-35%. I figured each ingredient of a particular sandwich or breakfast or dinner, and knew what it would cost to serve each plate. By doing this, I was able to monitor weekly the profit or loss of each restaurant and bar. My responsibility was to control the cost of food and beverages only. The labor and operating cost were the responsibility of the Director of Food and Beverages. I found specializing in this part of the hotel industry to be very interesting.

There were many other incidents while at the Holiday Inn; my most memorable was meeting the owner of the hotel. On one very special day, a bartender did not show up for work when the hotel had a travel agent reception. I was asked to take over for the bartender. As a Food and Beverage Controller, I had to know what went into each cocktail for costing purposes, so it was easy for me to adapt to the situation for a day. A gentleman came unsteadily over to the bar and requested a whiskey. He looked like Colonel Sanders, of Kentucky Fried Chicken. He did not request a brand name at the time, so I just poured out a non-brand name whiskey. He took a sip and immediately said, "Son, when I ask for whiskey, I expect to be served Jack Daniels.

I replied "Sorry Sir," with a smile, then said, "I will gladly change your drink" which I did.

He said, "Thank you," then wobbled back over to join the group of travel agents.

Another member from the management team noticed what had happened and came over. He said, "Do you know who that was? That was Mr. Wilson, the owner of the hotel." Of course I knew the name, but I had never met him in person before. Most of my controlling of sales and expense was behind the scenes and not directly customer-related. I then thought, "I wonder if the owner was testing me out to see how I would handle the situation?" I then thought, "I believe I would have passed the test."

Eventually, I was promoted to Assistant Purchasing Manager in charge of ordering all other supplies: Housekeeping, linens, shampoos, conditioners, china, silverware, you name it, everything that you would need to purchase to operate an efficient hotel. This meant dealing with every major purveyor and distributor on the island. This was a major responsibility. I enjoyed every moment of being a Food and Beverage Controller and the diversity of it. It not only involved accounting procedures, but working in and out of every restaurant and bar in the hotel; however, I appreciated the advancement. I was only twenty four and now the Assistant Purchasing Manager of the Holiday Inn. It was the newest and one of the most prestigious hotels on the island.

While still working at the hotel, I began dating the girl who would eventually become my wife. Her name was Helene. One day she came to visit me at my home. As I sat outside on my step on that beautiful sunny day, I was trying to play a trumpet. Needless to say, trying to learn how to play a trumpet did not last long. It was not my instrument; the guitar was. It gave me more flexibility to continue to write songs.

As we sat and talked for a while, my shield was let down, as they say. Jan and I no longer were together. I was feeling lonely; however, I was not ready for a long-term relationship. The conversation with the girl was rather spooky. You never know who's watching!

I used to sail my Sunfish sailboat on my days off, mostly in St. David's harbor. Helene told me, during our conversation, that she had often sat on the shoreline, watching me from a distance. She had become interested and intrigued. I used to sail all alone in the harbor in stormy seas. She found it to be scary watching, but yet exciting. Try to imagine a surfer in Hawaii or some other famous place for surfing. The most exciting time to surf is when a storm is coming in the distance. The seas begin to get rough, and the wind gets very strong. Surfers travel to far destinations to find remote spots for the thrill of riding the BIG wave. Sailing a boat in high winds is like wind surfing. Instead of standing holding the sail, you sit on the stern, (at the back.) You let the sail out until it balloons from the strong wind. The sail boat slides along the surface like a high speed powerboat. The difference is there's no loud power-motor sound. You just feel the wind and sea spray cooling your sun-burnt face.

Looking behind, you see a long white snowy trail of wake marking your path.

I have always reveled in challenges and excitement. There I was, a young man, living on a tropical island surrounded by sea. This was my play ground. I did not surf, but I loved to sail in stormy weather, long before it became a hurricane. I struggled, sailing against the strong wind, to reach the entrance of the harbor, and after reaching the entrance, I turned to fly across the water with the gale-force wind behind me straining my sail, as fast as the boat would go, bellowing through the rough seas. I never thought for a moment of the danger. It was just so exciting to do. When I reached the end of the harbor, I bailed out the water and started all over again. While this was all going on, she was sitting on the shore, in a secluded area in the brush, just watching. I never knew at the time that anyone was watching. It was just me, against the stormy sea. I played tennis on my days off as well, and I wondered if she was watching me then, also.

Our relationship grew because she often purposely missed the school bus. She usually traveled on the bus to get to high school. She was seventeen, in her senior year and about to graduate. The school was close to the Holiday Inn where I worked. She was at the bus-stop mostly every morning having 'missed' the bus. I picked her up on my way to work and gave her a ride to school. On weekends she worked in a restaurant near the hotel, in the old town of St. George's. Holiday Inn was only a few minutes outside of town. One day, she borrowed a small 50cc motor bike from a friend, and brought me a freshly cooked, local fish sandwich. I was a young executive and had the privilege to eat in the hotel; however, I felt the attention was rather special, and nobody cooked fresh, local fish like the islanders. On her way back to the restaurant, it began to rain. The road was very slippery. It was a dangerous time to be riding a bike. While turning on a slippery corner, she had a very bad accident, and the bike slipped from under her. She broke her leg. I felt responsible that day because she had come to see me at work to bring me a special treat.

We continued to see each other, but things became complicated. Bermuda was experiencing a lack of young, upcoming hotel executives. There were many times I scanned the hotel employment advertisements in the local paper. It was frustrating, because many positions in the job market advertised that only foreign employees need apply; this was very unfair. There were many qualified local people, but the hotels wanted white Europeans or Americans in executive positions.

In an advertisement, I saw that the Sonesta Beach Hotel needed a Food and Beverage Controller. It was a much larger hotel than Holiday Inn. I pondered whether I should make such a major career change. After giving it much thought, I realized that this move would not only affect my career but my personal life as well. When the band folded at the end of the year in 1973, I had moved back to St. David's and was living with my cousin, Gail, and her husband, Tommy. We shared a beautiful home overlooking St.

David's harbor. The home was very near other relatives and friends who had all grown up together.

Our grandmother had recently died. My grandfather had died a few years previously. The family was now moving in different directions. After my grandfather and grandmother passed, the family, in many ways, separated to pursue their own goals. Although some of the families moved on in different directions, many of us stayed together and made an effort to remain connected. The Fox Family, even though we live in different areas of the islands and abroad, have continued to be very close in our relationships. It was a bond we have shared through the generations. Today, after many years of raising our own families, we are still in contact. However, our family bond was put to the test for my mother and me, personally.

When my grandfather died, an official Will, written in the presence of a lawyer as they do today, was not available. He had hand-written his desire on pieces of ordinary paper. My youngest aunt, Lydia (Diddles), who had seven children, (Leah, Gerry, Wanda, Paris, David, Penny and Chanel) was to have the main homestead; my oldest aunt, Gloria, who also had seven children, (Toppy, Gail, Chris, Tony, Gregory and Patricia) was to keep her existing home. My mother, who only had me, was to keep her existing home. My grandfather felt his sons, Harry, who had three children (Wayne, Sheena and Leo) and his other son Ivan, who only had one son, (Linden) were financially okay and had their own homes so needed no further legacy than his blessing. Their sisters were the ones needing what grandfather had to give.

This did not turn out according to my grandfather's wish. In those days, if the Will was not accepted by the probate court, the oldest son, inherited. Grandfather's Will, written on ordinary sheets of paper, was not valid according to the so- called Laws of the land. Despite her father's express and clearly written desires, my mother and her sisters lost their homes because the holistic Will he had left was not deemed legal and valid, and Uncle chose not to honor his father's wishes and took full advantage of his windfall. Harry received all the inheritance. He soon took possession of all the property.

The first to be demolished to make room for a large estate was my mother's little wooden house. I say little, referring to today's standard size of home, but it was comfortable. It had two bedrooms, a kitchen, bathroom and a small living room. In those days, there were no separate deeds for each little home. They were just added to the existing estate as the family grew. It broke my mother's heart to see her house destroyed, even though we no longer lived in the little house at the time. Harry, my mother's eldest brother, then pursued the purchase of the house Gail, Tommy and I were renting, which was for sale. He, now, had the old homestead my grandfather had left for his daughters and his present home as collateral to purchase. I suppose he wanted to purchase the house because it was newer than his present one. It was also in a better location.

The house was overlooking the harbor where his boat was moored. At the time, it was disappointing for me, but instead of looking at it as a discouragement, I looked at it as an opportunity to move on to a new experience. Tommy was in the Air Force and was about to be discharged, so he and my cousin Gail were about to move to the United States. Everything seemed to come to a boil at the same time. The opportunity for me to leave was logical.

The Sonesta Beach Hotel was located on the far western end of the island in Southampton Parish. The position at the Sonesta Beach Hotel required a specialized person. I was certified, so I applied for the position. Partly, my motive was to prove that a Bermudian native could successfully fill a management position. When I was promoted, I had always trained a Bermudian to take over my position, so I felt if I did this once again, I would be free to move on.

Despite my heritage, my training and experience were persuasive. My application was accepted, so I now had to relocate, out of St. David's. This also meant that the relationship with Helene could possibly come to an end.

To my surprise, this is where my relationship with her seriously began. She had already graduated and was working full-time at a restaurant. She was determined that she did not want to end the relationship, so she decided she would leave home and follow me. As it turned out, we broke the establishment's cardinal rule; we lived together for a few months before we realized that we should get married, and so we did.

I found myself in a complicated relationship. At first, her mother did not want us to get married. Her family was Seventh Day Adventist. I had grown up in the Church of England, an Anglican church. I had already left the church because of a racial encounter, but now I was facing religious differences. After careful thought, I became a Seventh Day Adventist as well. Her parents then gave consent to the marriage.

Although Bermuda was very integrated, there was still some very real racial and religious diversity. The island had the most diverse churches in the western hemisphere. Every church you can think of could be found in the tiny communities of Bermuda. It was only twenty-one miles long and two and a half miles wide. Most of the communities worshiped on Sunday; others worshiped on Saturday (The Seventh Day Adventist). The most common churches were African Methodist, Episcopal, Church of England and Catholic. Bermuda, as beautiful as it is on the outside, had a lot of tension on the inside.

Tourists only saw the beauty of the island's physical appearance; of course, one could not blame them. They had enough of these social and religious problems at home. It was a time in United States when President John F. Kennedy, an Irish Catholic, and Martin Luther King, a Black Baptist, were dealing with school integration problems. For a small island, we were no different than the rest of the world.

Some unchristian members of church congregations can turn people away from God and His Church. My experience, at the age of eighteen, caused me to leave the Church of England. Later in my life, I forgave the congregation, because I came to realized that the real message to be heard is from God Himself, through His Son Jesus Christ and The Holy Spirit. At the time, though, it shook my faith.

When I was born, my mother took me to the Chapel of Ease, Church of England (Anglican) in St. David's. It was there I was christened Jay David Kent Fox. We worshipped on Sunday. I continued in the church until I turned eighteen, in the year, 1967. During that time, I was a youth leader and sang as a choir boy. I was also an altar boy. As altar boys, we shared the honor of carrying the cross in a traditional Anglican service. The boy who arrived first in the morning had the reward of carrying the cross. It was a privilege, a traditional illustration of how Jesus Christ, Our Lord and Savior, had carried the cross before he was crucified and died for all who had sinned. We also had communion service every Sunday morning. Altar boys had to be confirmed in order to assist the Priest in communion service. I was confirmed in the Cathedral in the city of Hamilton.

The youth, black and white, in the community got along wonderfully. We went to school together and played together. Racial problems were not an issue with the children. I found out as I got older; it was some of the parents who carried this disease, discrimination. I was at an age where I began to notice girls who had blossomed into beautiful ladies. It wasn't long before I became involved, dating a girl who also attended the same church. I was of an interracial family; the girl was not. Her father did not want an interracial family, so he instructed her never to see me again. Reluctantly, she ended the relationship. I, personally, felt scorned, so I ended my relationship with that church. I believed that there had been a false love in that church community for some folks and not others. It never was as it seemed. In those early years, I could not stand being surrounded by a church community which falsely claimed to love one another but actually felt scorn for people of different denominations or races. Although there were so many good Christians in the church, my aunts, uncles, cousins and close friends, this situation affected me deeply. In my heart, I was devastated, I felt history repeating itself. It was the same situation that my father and mother had faced twenty years previously. As a white Englishman, my father hated discrimination. He spoke out against the night clubs, restaurants and churches which discriminated against people. He would immediately leave, with my mother's hand in his. He and his friends would no longer be customers of that particular business. However, he had no control over the British military. He was eventually separated from my mother and relocated far away against his will, permission to marry refused by his military superiors.

I had been a single, free-spirited, joyful entertainer. Now, at twenty five, I was beginning a new career, a new marriage, attending a new church, and within the same year of marriage, we had our first daughter, Julie, on August 18, 1974. Two years later we had our second daughter, Rebecca, on February 24th, 1976. What a life-changing experience it seemed, trying to balance the world on my shoulders. However, there was a wonderful distraction. I now had two beautiful daughters. Oh what joy God had given me with these two girls. They were the pride of my life. Each day, I arrived home from work just to give them a big hug. The stress of my day would go immediately. I loved to take them to the park and beaches. We lived near Warwick Long Beach, on the beautiful south shore of the island. There is a perfect swimming area for children. It is called Jobson's Cove. It is an excellent place for children to learn to swim. The cove water was very shallow, warm, and safe.

The new job at the Sonesta Beach Hotel was very challenging, and the pay was excellent. Eventually, I was promoted to an assistant Food and Beverage Manager. It now required that I work longer hours and, many times, on our Sabbath. One evening, I was attending a revival at the Seventh Day Adventist Church. The speaker, well-known because of his appearances on a television program called "The Breath of Life," was named Charles Brooks. His topic that night was about making choices about where one should chose to work and what one should eat. We were told not to eat meat and to learn to eat vegetarian foods. We were also told not to work on the Sabbath. Friday evenings at sunset began the Seventh Day Adventist Sabbath which ended the following evening, at sunset. During those hours, it was suggested that no one should work. I knew all these things about the topic, because I had attended the church for eight years, and of course, Helene had grown up in the church. I, then, asked a member of the church a question, "Should I be a manager in a hotel?" Everyone understood that hotels were a 24 hour 7 day operation. Most of the population of Bermuda worked in the hotel industry. I also had to manage bars and nightclubs... The answer was, "No!" It was like a spear driven through my heart. I just could not give up my career, but I was deeply troubled.

It was at this revival I introduced the first inspirational song I had written, *I Came to Find My Jesus*. I loved the Lord, so I wrote how God had changed my life.

I'm just a stranger passing through this town.
I came to find my Jesus; I'm losing so much time.

I had continued playing my guitar, even though the band no longer existed. This revival was my first experience out of my familiar environment as a show-business entertainer. But, in this situation, I was not putting on a show; it was coming from my heart. It was just me and the guitar in front of 700 - 800 people. The song was very effective. I watched an elderly lady struggle her way through the crowd toward me after the service ended. She eventually, made it to the podium and reached out her hand to touch mine. At the same time, I reached down from the front of the stage and held her hand. With a kind face and gentle smile, she told me that she, "had to touch the messenger's hand," whom God had sent.

She commented on how much the song had touched her heart and lifted her spirit. I will never forget that moment in my life. I did not know, at the time, singing at that revival was the beginning of my music ministry. I wrote several inspirational songs during this period in 1977.

It took eighteen years to record them. Later in my journey, I learned that that had been one of God's calls to me. I did not know it, then. All I could hear ringing in my ear was, "No! You should not be working in bars and night clubs." Although I did not physically work as a bartender, it all came under my management responsibilities. With my beliefs, I had a difficult decision to make. It took me a long time to reconcile my responsibilities. When I was promoted, I was in charge of several restaurants, bars and night clubs, staffing and refurbishing of new equipment. I remained at the Sonesta Beach Hotel for a few more years. During my employment, I traveled to further my practical training, to Fort Lauderdale, Florida, Hartford, Connecticut and Boston in the chain of the Sonesta Hotels.

A few years later, the Food and Beverage Director, an Englishman named Michael Branch whom I assisted as F&B Manager, decided he wanted to move to Spain. He was offered a job managing a hotel there. He showed me photos of Spain and the hotel. It was a beautiful place. I did not discourage him for wanting a change. Mike and I worked very well together. I learned a lot from him. Instead of the hotel promoting me into the job for which I had extensively trained, they transferred a new Food and Beverage Director from the Sonesta Hotel in Boston, where I had trained, previously. I was disappointed in their decision. After a few months of working with the new director who had been brought in. I could no longer continue. His ethics and mine clashed very often. He was a very shrewd and a deceptive individual. He reminded me of a Mafia boss, appointed to be a manger from the casinos of Las Vegas. He looked as though he had come right out of one of those mob movies.

I had grown up in Bermuda and had, now, worked in hotel management for eight years. He had trouble communicating with Bermudian employees and any other employee for that matter. He had a very autocratic style. When he could not get his own way in one particular incident, he tried to manipulate me to fire an employee for no apparent valid reason. This particular employee had a squabble with his supervisor which was not work related. The manager's solution was to have me fire the lower level worker over what was essentially a minor personal issue. I felt that his solution was unfair and unnecessary. I refused and approached the president of the hotel about the director's ethics. My experience was that if a grievance was not handled correctly, you could have a major strike on your hands. Apparently, the contract of the new director gave him a lot of authority, and the president advised me to work with him despite the ethical questions. I, eventually, resigned, because I could not approve of his management tactics, and could no longer work under those conditions for a man I could neither like nor respect.

THE BIRTHDAY PARTY

An opportunity came for me to manage a small club, restaurant, bar and cottage complex, known as The Pompano Beach Club and Cottage Colony. I was, again, successful in my application. I put my heart and soul into my work. I took opportunities to continue to educate myself further in hotel management. I, now, had experience in several departments. This position included the management of all accounts, front desk, and maintenance, the beauty of the property and oversight of guest relations.

One evening, there was a late plane arrival, so I had to check in the reservation, myself. The front desk manager and bell staff had already finished their shifts. A gentleman was travelling alone. When he finally arrived at the hotel, I checked him in. I told him I would show him to his room. The cottages were separated from the main club house. He had had a few drinks on his flight and was feeling no pain. He was well-dressed, in a suit, so it seemed to me that he was a guy who was so stressed out from working, knowing that he was going on vacation, that he had just let all caution go to the wind. This was no motel; it was a luxury resort and not cheap, so I knew he must have a good job and was not normally a drunk. I took his bags and asked him to follow me. He wobbled toward the exit door behind me. After a few minutes of him following me, I was in motion, turning to tell him his room was only a few steps ahead. When I turned and looked, he had disappeared. I dropped the bags and walked back to find him. There he was, passed out in the flower garden, as if he was sleeping on a cloud. I know we kept the gardens and walkways beautiful, but heaven it was not. Thankfully, he was not dead. I grabbed his arm and placed it over my shoulder and struggled getting him to his room. He was not a huge man, but a guy in this condition is dead weight and heavy. I finally got him settled. I'm sure he did not remember a thing the next day, but I did. I thought it was hilarious, and never will forget.

A most incredible event happened at this time of my life. It was a beautiful day, August 18, 1977. We were having a birthday party for Julie, my daughter. What was to be just a birthday, turned out to be the start of the adventure of a lifetime and, for me personally, a miracle!

The celebration began at my home, with family, friends and their children. The children were laughing and playing. The sun was shining; not a cloud was in the sky. It was still very much a summer day in Bermuda. The temperature was high, in the 80's. Over the background of children laughing and playing, you could hear conversations of parents saying, "Oh, how their little girl has grown. She looks just like her father." and another, "She looks a little more like her mother." So the conversations went. Personally, I felt Julie looked a little like both her mother and me. Later, I went into the house and picked up the family album to see photos of Helene and me when we were young. The photos included our parents. As I lifted it and turned the pages, I focused on a photo of my father. It was taken November 24th, 1950. He was dressed in his military uniform. He was tall and slim, with dark hair. He had a tattoo on his left arm just below his elbow. He had soft eyes and a narrow, pointed nose. The photo was in black and white, so I could not see the color of his eyes. I knew his eyes were blue because my Mom had told me. Julie's eyes are blue; neither Helene nor I had blue eyes.

The photo had been taken while he was stationed in Malaysia. It was sent to my Mother, among other photos of him in his military uniform and casual attire. It was this photo of my Father that made me realize who Julie really resembled. She had his facial features and his blue eyes. I was amazed how incredibly she looked like her grandfather, my Dad. It was then that I began to gaze at the ceiling and wonder if my father was alive. On the back of the photo, he had written the location, year, and date, and a message to my mother that read, "To Singer, with all my love, Harry." He had marked twenty-one 'x s' known as kisses. One for each year he had lived...interesting, I thought. My grandfather had called Mother 'Singer' because she was always singing wherever and whatever she was doing. Apparently, my father had agreed.

After everyone had left and the party was over, my wife and I sat down and came to a conclusion. The question that lingered in my mind was, "Is my Dad still alive?" An unsolved mystery hungered in my heart. For the many years, as I grew up from a young boy to a teenager, I had wished my father was there. My wife and I discussed how we could go about solving this mystery. To begin, we made a promise that, if he was alive, we would not cause problems with his present situation. Our lives had been very prosperous over the years. We had our own home, car, boat, traveled a lot and our lives were a little above average. We did not need a thing other than to know whether or not my father was alive.

I was now 28 years of age, and it seemed a whole life-time had passed by.

Jay's Father, Harold Savage, November 24th, 1950

From Mom's shoe-box, pictures of Jay and his Dad.

To begin this search for my father, we got out my mom's old shoe box with all of the treasures she had kept, including photos of my dad, baby photos of me and letters he had written. She had given me this box, long ago. The letters found in the shoebox held special memories my mother and my father had shared together. My mother had received letters from my father for a period of three years after he had to leave Bermuda. Reading the letters, I could feel that my father had become depressed from being apart from my mother and the son he never got to see. When he had to leave Bermuda, he became so unhappy that he even began to rebel against his senior officers.

On several occasions, with the extra money he earned while stationed in Malaysia, he had sent gifts of clothing to my mother for me. Among these little treasures in the shoe box, folded neatly, was a silk baby outfit with tiny new-born baby shoes my dad had sent with a birthday card. The birthday card was a one-fold, carved mother teddy bear holding a tiny teddy bear. On the inside, the card read on the left, "I'll bet you think, because I'm so small I just can't love you much at all..." on the right side it read, "But really, you should look inside-my heart is awful BIG and WIDE. At the end was a heart with two flowers. In the middle of a heart was DADDY. The card was signed, "To baby Jay, from Daddy."

There was something significant about his signature which became his trade mark. Before signing his name, he put a forward slash above a capital "T" and a forward slash below the "o" before writing a note, than signed his name, Daddy or Harry. This is interesting, because it had become the way I sign autographs or cards. He ended his signature with a period. Every time I sign my signature, I end it with a period, too. I was unaware of this. This was pointed out to me by my life-insurance agent. When I had to sign a document, he looked for the dot at the end of my signature. He, then, showed me this in all my previous signatures. There were many times Dad would print his words. I print everything I write. These little comparisons in our lives become intriguing later on.

My wife and I were hoping to find an old address or something that my mom had used to send letters to him. Eventually, we did find an address for a Nicholas street in Ardwick, Manchester, England. We made many attempts to find him, but to no avail. Excitement began to build. One night, when my wife and I were watching "Magnum PI" starring Tom Sellick, an idea came upon me; I said, "Why don't we hire a private investigator?"

On September 19th' 1977, I contacted Island-Wide Security Ltd. The cost was only fifty dollars. The investigating company had a contact in Chudleigh Road, Manchester, named B.E.T. Ellison. The company must have contacted their source the same day we hired them, because they copied me a letter from them dated September 27th, 1977. Within a matter of nine days, their mission was complete. It's overwhelming for me, looking at the details as I'm writing this story. When all this was happening, the excitement took precedent over all the details. Thankfully, I'm a person who keeps all paper work of importance.

I was at work late one night at the hotel, doing payroll, when the phone rang. It was the principal investigator of Island- Wide Security; he asked for me. When I said it was I speaking, he said, "Mr. Fox, we have found your father!" I, in a state of shock, went speechless. He told me that inquiries had been made in Nicholas Street, Ardwick, Manchester, but it was found that the street was now situated in the middle of a demolition area. All the houses in that street, together with the surrounding property, had been pulled down several years previous. Further inquiries were made in the locality, but it was not possible to obtain any information concerning Mr. Harold Savage, my dad. Following further extensive inquiries, it was ascertained that my father now resided in Stone Ridge, Hadfield, Hyde, Cheshire, approximately fifteen miles from Manchester. The Manchester contact's assistant had spoken to my father and confirmed that he was the person whom we were seeking. My father was, naturally, curious to know who was trying to contact him and wanted to hear from that person.

Shortly after I received the call, the President of Pompano Beach Hotel came in my office and saw me in a state of shock. He asked if I was okay. "Did you just hear bad news?" Little did he know I had just heard GREAT NEWS!! I told him what just had happened, and for me, it was too incredible to believe. The principal of Island-Wide Security had given me a phone number to contact my dad if we so wished. I returned home, late that night after work, and told my wife what had happened. I handed her the phone number which the Investigator had given me. She, surprised about the discovery, did not stop there. England was several hours ahead of Bermuda, and by her calculations, it was morning where my father lived. She took the phone number which I had given her, and she began to call the number. I reminded her that we had promised not to intervene. She then said, "Don't you want to know more? You must be curious." That I was, but did not know what to do. I went into the bedroom; she remained in the living room and continued to make the call. From the bedroom, I could hear that she had made the connection and was having a conversation with whom-ever was on the other end of the phone line. At this point, I could not stand the curiosity any longer, so I picked up the extension phone. At that very moment, I heard my father say, for the first time in my life, "Where is Jay?" I answered as if it had been said a million times or more, "I'm here, Dad."

We talked for awhile...small talk. I don't remember the exact conversation, but, for sure, it was getting acquainted, about who's who, my family, his family and what had happened as the years went by. He said that things after the war had been very bad in Manchester, so he had remained home to help take care of his parents. He explained how England was in a financial depression. It was difficult to raise enough money to return to Bermuda. He told me that the correspondence with my mother had stopped. My mother later explained that, since we lived in a rural area in St. David's, often the mail would get lost because of high winds, or the children would interfere with it. We did not have secure mail boxes those days. The mailman delivered the mail right to the door. When no one was home, he left the mail outside the door between stones, easy for mischievous children to find.

My father said that he had gotten married, after he lost contact with my mother, and had started a family. I found that I had a half-brother and two half-sisters. Their names were Marsha, Michael and Gail. My father had told his wife, Pat, about having a son in Bermuda, but he had never recalled telling the children. Within a few weeks, letters began to flow back and forth. My dad was not much at writing letters, so most of the correspondence was written by Pat. The first letter ended by reading. "Love, Pat, or should I say, Mom." It was a warm feeling to know that she sincerely cared, was glad that I had contacted my father and that, rather than resenting me, she welcomed me into her life.

Most of the letters shared back and forth were of birthday wishes, holiday greetings and anniversaries. Photos were also exchanged. On one occasion, I sent a photo of myself and a long bio, describing my life as a young boy to an adult. My father had received the photo and letter. After reading it, he left it on the dining room table. One of my sisters passed by the table and saw the photo. Curiously, she asked, "Dad, is that a photo of you when you were young?" The resemblance between my father and me was remarkable. There was no denying that I was his son. I guess at this point, he gathered the family together and told them the whole story about being stationed in Bermuda and meeting a young native girl, telling them that he and she were about to be married when he was sent off to Malaysia to prevent it. We received a letter describing this conversation, and my father expressed how he was worried how the children would take it. They were grown, young adults. Mike and Marsha were in their early 20's. Gail, the youngest, was in her late teens. Marsha was the most excited one, finding out she had a big brother, living on a romantic island.

At the beginning stages of all these events, my biological mother was very ill in the hospital. She did not live with my wife and me at the time. She lived in an apartment about 5 miles away from us. She was very independent and worked in a major hotel nearby before getting ill. She had her own transportation and visited with the family often. While she was recovering in the hospital, I visited her daily. During a visit, I told her of the news of finding my father. At first I did not want to tell her while she was in hospital, not knowing how she'd react. However, I could not hold back the good news. Before telling her the news, thoughts went through my mind. "If I tell her while she is in hospital about finding my father, would it make her more ill than she is; would it burst her bubble? Did she ever think, in her own mind, that my father would return to Bermuda?" As I began to tell my mother the news, she was incredibly understanding and most happy for me. How she felt, I would never know. Her personal feelings were kept to herself. She was happy that I would finally get to know my father in person.

THE INSPIRATION TO
WRITE THIS STORY

This is how this story book romance all began. At first, my mind wandered in complete imagination. In my mind, I imagined adventurers of the sea and Pirates. Two young adults, a girl and a boy about twenty, trapped on a tropical island. The scene was similar to the movie, "The Blue Lagoon," starring Brooke Shields. However, a switch went off in my head, and I was back to reality. The phone call had been made. The detective had reported, and I had the first letter from my father in my hand. I had read it, but it was precious. I was at work and had taken 'The Letter' with me to savor the moment of getting to know my father. I began to answer his questions on just a small post card, but I could not stop writing. I tore up the post card and began to write a letter. In the letter, I wrote how children understood things today, like relationships, divorce, separations, death, etc. I continued writing and exploring the situation on paper. I was so excited I wrote an autobiography of my life from a young boy to an adult. I wrote about my wife, children and becoming a hotel executive. I enclosed in the letter photos of my youth and entertainment career in a popular band.

In my father's situation, the challenge was war, which separates people. Long distance relationships seldom survive. In a war-torn country like Britain, financial depression sets in, and things get tough for everyone. My mother had not received his letters, so she had written none. He had to put that life behind him, and moved on. This first attempt to work the situation out on paper was the beginning of this book. Their story was a real-life romance.

He must have handled the surprise about me well, because within a year, Marsha, my half sister, was the first to arrive in Bermuda to meet me, personally. Marsha arrived in Bermuda, and immediately became part of the family. God had made things so easy for us and natural. Nothing seemed awkward or uncomfortable. It was wonderful to share our way of life in Bermuda with my new-found sister. Like everyone visiting the beautiful semi-tropical island of Bermuda, we went to the beach. We had such a beautiful day there; the water sparkled like crystals. It was such a magical sight to see when our heads were level with surface of the ocean. Later, the excitement of enjoying the day with Marsha inspired me to write a song entitled *Crystal Waters*.

My imagination went wild. Reflecting on the day, I could see an orchestra playing. As the water hit the coral shore line it crashed high into the air, like clashing cymbals in a musical symphony. The sun sparkled on the surface of the ocean like dazzling diamonds. I could hear chimes, and violins playing. Our almighty God was the conductor. Only He could create such a glorious scene. The first line of my song expresses my feelings: I was so overwhelmed with its beauty. Even though I had grown up with this atmosphere, it would never grow old. I loved my home. I could not wait until the next day to go swimming and diving again.

Crystal waters, and shining sun; Wake me up... when morning comes.

For an entertainer and song writer, Bermuda was a great place to live my fantasies. Thus, I had written many songs inspired by the way of life.

Jay sings *Jenny*, playing his twelve string guitar

My first daughter, Julie, inspired me to write a song I titled *Jenny*. Many songs I had written over the years were eventually performed on my twelve-string guitar. The song is a story about a daddy's little girl. Julie was about four. As I sat on my bed trying to write a song, nothing was coming, no picture, no imagination, no melody, absolutely nothing; my mind was blank. I learned later that you can't force inspiration to come out of you. I was frustrated. Suddenly, Julie came running in the bed room crying, after falling off her bike. She had been riding outside in the driveway. My first reaction was, "Don't bother me; Daddy is trying to write a song." At that moment, I was crushed about what I had just said. I gasped, my hand over my mouth, catching myself. I realized that, in the moment of frustration, I had almost ignored her. She looked up at me with her beautiful, blue eyes, tears trickling down her face. My body quivered. Her whole life flashed before me. I imagined that I saw her in an open field, bobbing joyfully through yellow daisies. She was dressed in a blue dress with a white, lace collar around the neck. My wife had purchased for it her. You could barely see her in the distance. She was hopping through the tall flowers, about knee high, coming toward me. As she got closer and closer, she was getting bigger and bigger. When she finally reached me, she was a grown woman, now dressed in a wedding gown. Then, I saw myself looking into her bed room where I had kissed her good night...it was empty. In my room, at this very moment, my body shook; I dropped my guitar on the bed and stood up quickly. Immediately, I reached down, arms out-stretched and picked her up, snuggling her to my chest tightly. The comfort and security of my embrace took her tears away instantly. I suddenly realized that I must pay attention to my little girl. She would grow up very quickly. Through this scene, my mind was now filled with a story I must write down. It became the song *Jenny* it was recorded and responsible for selling hundreds of copies of my first album.

Visions and circumstances always captured my mind. I had many times written a line or two to document a moment. One day I wrote a song titled *silently*. Lying in the grass on a hillside on that beautiful sunny afternoon, hands clasped behind my head, looking up at the sky, I felt peaceful and quiet. I thought to myself, "It's so silent I could hear a cloud passing by." I then thought, "What a great poetic line for a song."

While Marsha was in Bermuda, my wife and I took her to several of the popular night spots and fine restaurants. She and I went to the historic part of Bermuda, where the first voyages shipwrecked and discovered the islands in the Old Town of St. George's. We also traveled that day to St. David's where I grew up and the Battery where our father had been stationed. In St.

David's, we, eventually, met many relatives and friends our father had traveled with, and he had grown to love. She found out quickly why it was so easy for our father, a young soldier, to feel so at home, away from home. I'm sure many soldiers can relate to that situation, especially in times of war.

America is in conflict again, now, in Iraq and Afghanistan, as I write this story. The soldiers who are fighting are going through what my father went through, leaving families behind, some never returning and some returning to find that their lives have been changed drastically, forever. Others return home to live a prosperous life.

After a few weeks' stay, Marsha returned to England. She had met her extended family and was ready to take the news back home. The letters began to flow again, and then suddenly, there was no communication for quite some time. I began to be concerned and thought we had said or done something wrong. However, my sixth sense was telling me something different. I called to find out if everything was okay. Pat answered the phone. In a soft voice she told me, "Your father caught pneumonia and has been admitted to hospital." He was held there in very critical condition. The family in England had not known how to tell me this. I had just found my father. This was why they were afraid to let me know the situation, hoping that he would recover before I found out.

My first reaction was, "Oh God, do not let this happen now, not until I get the chance to meet my father in person." At this point in my life, like most young couples, I had debt up to my ears. I had a mortgage to pay, a new car, living expenses; you name it. That did not stop what I had in mind to do. I went directly to Penboss, a travel agency in the city of Hamilton. I told them the story of just finding my father after not knowing him for the first twenty-eight years of my life. I had, thank God, good credit. The travel agency advanced me tickets to travel to England. I purchased two, one for me and the other for Julie, my daughter. She was the one who had inspired this whole effort to find my father, so I felt it only right to take her along on this journey. She was age 4 at the time. My wife stayed home with our other daughter, Rebecca, and worried. In a few days, we boarded the flight on British Airways and headed for England. It was a long flight.

In 1978, England had the worst snow storm they had had in many years. When we arrived at Heathrow airport in London, it was still snowed in. No connecting flights were going to Manchester, so we had to take a train. What an adventure. We traveled hills and valleys, passed sheep farms, all covered in snow. It was a beautiful sight, traveling through the countryside of old England. It was very cold outside; Julie and I were dressed in very warm clothing which had been bought for this trip. Of course, we had not needed it in Bermuda.

We arrived in Manchester and had to transfer from one train to another to get to Hadfield, via Hyde, Cheshire. By this time, Julie was very tired from all the travel and transfers from the plane to two other trains. She fell asleep on my shoulder. I had a bag in one hand, a guitar the other and my child in the third, so you can imagine, I was struggling. I had brought along my guitar, because my father and I had music in common. He loved to sing at functions and at pubs in the local area. We sang most of the same songs, a surprise we had discovered through our previous correspondence.

Suddenly, my prayers were answered. It so happened that the world-famous Manchester United Soccer Team was on the train. Martin Buchan, I found out by introduction, was the captain of the team. He offered to help with my dilemma. Martin held Julie in his arms and helped her on and off the train. I thanked him, and he had a photo session with Julie. David McCreey and Brian Greenhoff, two other members of the soccer team, helped with the guitar and luggage bag. Wow! This was amazing, from what I learned after getting to the house, later. No one at the house or anyone they knew had ever met Martin, personally. He was like the Super Bowl hero, quarter-back Tom Brady, of the New England Patriots.

Manchester United Soccer Team was celebrating a century in the sport and was headed to a big match on the weekend. I got to see the game between them and Manchester City during our stay. What an exciting match that was. One gentlemen fan of Manchester United, sitting behind me, kept yelling out "Go Reds! Go Reds!" the name fans had given to the club. Suddenly, a Manchester United forward player shot a goal. The ball went in and out of the goal so fast. The guy who was yelling so much had annoyed others, so someone tried to hush up him up. When he turned to respond to that, the enthusiastic fan missed the exciting goal. He yelled, "What happened?" Of course, the poor guy was disappointed he had missed seeing the goal, but was happy his soccer team, Manchester United, had won the match. No one knew that my daughter had been in the arms of the hero whose team-mate kicked the winning goal.

We finally arrived in Hadfield. There, at the train station, Marsha was waiting. It was exciting to see her again but more exciting to encounter what was about to happen. We traveled through the wintery, narrow streets of Hadfield and, finally, arrived at the house. There still was lots of snow on the ground that led up to the front door. They must have heard the car pull in the drive-way. The door opened slowly and, standing at the open door, was my father, wearing a bath robe, over his clothing for additional warmth. The pneumonia he had caught had finally cleared up. It was a moment of deep emotion, finally meeting his first son for the first time. He stood at the door with his arms open wide. I stood there standing, at six foot three, like a towering basketball player. He said, "Hi, son; long time no see" and gave me a BIG HUG! I was in my father's arms for the first time. We all gathered around in the family room, with the fire burning, getting acquainted. The home was just a simple, wonderful, little country cottage, nestled in the heart of Hadfield, England.

The next morning, my father was feeling a lot better, so he dressed warmly and headed out the door to make a snowman with his first granddaughter, my daughter Julie. It was hard to believe he was feeling that good, to go out in the cold. I guess the excitement of the moment would make anyone forget he was ever as sick as he had been.

That evening, it was my turn. The family took me to an old pub to play pool. My dad was the pool champion in the area, and he wanted to show off his skills. I tried to play a little. I hardly had time to learn how to be a great pool player, but I really enjoyed seeing my father play and the big smile on his face as he was winning yet another challenge. I did get to sing that night; I sang *Day Dream Believer,* a big hit in England originally recorded by *The Monkees..* They also had a hit TV Show many years ago.

I soon had to return to Bermuda after the wonderful experience of uniting with my father and meeting my extended family. But, after returning home, and sharing the excitement of seeing my father with Helene, sadly, our personal lives began to rapidly crumble. She felt that she had grown up in a very strict environment in the church. She had decided to explore what the worldly life had to offer. Our marriage was falling apart. After six years of a happy beginning and sharing the best gift of our lives, two beautiful daughters, our marriage had become very troubled.I blamed myself many times because I was a young man who had spent a lot of time building a career in the hotel industry. My life had changed so rapidly within a short period of time. I must admit, I did not understand the importance of balancing a career, a marriage, a family, the purchase of a new home, and a religion which told me I could not work in the career I had chosen. This lack of balance began to cause problems; my heavy work load took a toll on our marriage. She worked at an insurance company in the city of Hamilton and had work stresses of her own. In addition to working, she had the challenges of being the mother of two, the wife of a very busy husband and the growing conviction that she wanted more and different things.

The stress and pressures of having to work on Sabbath, even though I was very committed to the church and had become a Sabbath School Teacher, became over-whelming. I had decisions to make. I could not give up my career at the time, and I could not meet the requirements of the church. My wife and I were soon separated. Helene and little Rebecca went to St. David's to live with her parents. Within the two years of separation, we tried to reconcile and correct our mistakes, but this trial period floundered and became very difficult for us both. We failed to solve the problems, so we filed for a divorce. I thought to myself, "I have been going to church and trying to bring up my children the correct way, and yet, my marriage has ended anyway." I became very discouraged and no longer attended any congregation, or worship service. I had tried so hard and felt that life had failed me. I was thirty-two, and my life was shattered. When the divorce became final, Helene was awarded custody of the girls. But, Julie remained with me for a short time. She was six and had begun school. We did not want her to have to change schools so soon. My mother, moved in with me to help care for her. My other daughter, Rebecca, was only four at the time and had been taken with her mother. I did not want the girls to be separated, so eventually, Julie joined her sister. I thought the girls would continue to go to the elementary school where Helene and I had both attended, but things suddenly changed drastically. Helene had met someone and was going to marry him. She took the girls over to the United States, to San Diego. They lived in Chula Vista, California. This was thousands of miles from Bermuda. How could I see my children? I felt I had lost the joy of my life, my daughters. I had to accept that Helene was beginning a new life. Later, after they were settled, I flew over to San Diego to visit them. The distance was so far away from Bermuda, I could not visit them often. Eventually, they moved to Florida, on the Gulf coast, and I was able to visit them more frequently, but not often enough, as I later learned.

My personal life style began to change as well. My marriage had defaulted, and my daughters were no longer with me. I cried for weeks. It was my cousin Gerry who had married my drummer, Leroy Jones from *The Variations*, who pulled me together. I stayed out very late. I saw few sun rises, went to discos and went into a careless lifestyle, totally changing my pattern of work, home, family and church. I don't know how, but I was still able to focus on my job.

IT TAKES A VILLAGE
TO GET IT RIGHT

While managing at the Pompano Hotel I rediscovered my first love, as a guitarist and entertainer. Late one evening, I was doing payroll and realized that I was paying the entertainer, Stan Seymour, more in one night than I was making in almost a week. Of course, he was a night-club star and brought in the business. Stan was an excellent entertainer and had a few island hits. His most famous song was, *The Diddley Bops and the Goose-Neck Handle Bars.* It was a fun song about teenagers and their careless style of riding their motor bikes, zigzagging through the motor cars. You may not remember it, but it was a big hit in Bermuda that year. I remember the movie *Easy Rider* starring Peter Fonda, Jack Nicholson and Dennis Hopper. They rode their motor bikes with long goose-neck handle bars; the Bermuda teenagers and their bikes were very much the same. Stan wrote original songs and entertained the guests, telling about the fun, cultural side of the island. He was also the entertainer who made me realize that I should carry on the tradition of island entertainers. Tourist loved the Caribbean music and rhythm of the island. I had night club experience as well but had given up playing in a band to develop my hotel management career, fulltime.

Entertainers only performed part-time during the evening. They usually worked another job during the day. Being a manager took up all my time, day and night. I came to work at 8 AM and stayed until noon. At 6 PM, I returned for the evening shift staying until 1 AM to close out the evening business and lock up. I realized that I was selling myself short and now rediscovered the thing I loved the most, playing the guitar and performing. I knew I needed something in my life to lift my spirit once again. I resigned my management job at Pompano Beach Hotel and Cottage Colony. I sought a job which would allow me to work during the day, so I could get back into entertaining at night.

I made myself available and was immediately booked in hotels as an entertainer. How wonderful it was to be cradled back in my music again. I began singing popular island songs, such as *Bermuda Is Another World,* a melodic song written by a well-known entertainer on the island, the late Hubert Smith. The song describes the beauty and surroundings of the island, the coral, and the pink-speckled sand. I also sang songs from other famous island entertainers, such as *Yellow Bird,* the iconic song made widely recognized by Jamaica's Harry Belafonte. I sang many other popular songs, including my own. I became a sought-after entertainer for all ages. I made many fans over the years. They followed me all over the island to hear me sing. The songs and admiration of the fans were healing my wounds.

Over the years, I became so well-known that several hotels regularly booked me in their hotel night clubs and pubs. When visitors returned to the island for another vacation, they often traveled by a rented scooter or taxi from their hotel to where-ever I was performing on Bermuda.

On beautiful moonlight nights, the hotels had the entertainment out on the terrace overlooking the ocean. Others had their entertainment in the night-club, pub or piano lounge. One night, I was performing out on the terrace overlooking the secluded beach of The Reefs Hotel. The rhythm of my music captured the hearts of a couple walking on the beach below. They heard the music and decided to come up and dance. Later, we met, after my performance. They introduced themselves as Tom and Lois Sawtell from Guilford, Connecticut.

The Reefs Hotel restaurant also served dinner outside on the terrace. While people dined, they also danced near the music. Tom and Lois were an inspiring couple, and romantic to see, dancing under the stars. They became good friends. It was this couple who inspired me to write the song, *Like Magic,* because of this love-filled scene.

This particular night, I was exhausted after my performance. I had poured my heart and soul into the songs. After the show, I sat with the couple at their table to savor the moment. During our conversation, they told me they were celebrating their anniversary. They looked so happy.

"How do you sustain the romance?" I asked.

"We love each other," was their answer.

"There must be more!" I said.

They replied, "We keep the magic alive."

"Wow!" I thought, "Magic."

I returned home that night and picked up my guitar to write a love song. The words describe a love so powerful that separation was unimaginable. They had a quivering intimacy. They described the warmth of being together and sharing each-other's interests. It was a perfect fit, people experiencing an enduring love for each other. While writing the words and then playing the melody on my guitar, I had an emotional vibe from start to finish. I used chords which expressed the song so well.

I traveled to Cleveland, Ohio after the entertainment season to meet with my arranger, Bill Duncan. Bill and I collaborated in finishing the musical product. Everything seemed to mesh really well. Bill arranged all the music for the orchestra. In the end, we had a song arrangement we knew could be a hit.

Here are a few penned words of the song:

> *I can't imagine what would life be without you babe.*
> *I can't imagine what this world would be in that lifetime.*
> *I can't help it if you're like magic to me.*
> *I've lived this lifetime just waiting to love only you.*

Many of my fans not only came to see my performance, they also came to visit my home. I took them out in my boat for the day, at times. Often, they had me to their hotel for dinner. When they returned home, they sent me cards, letters and photos of their trip. When they returned to Bermuda, they brought me birthday gifts. Other fans made tee-shirts and buttons with my photo on them. I was a real celebrity to them. To me, I was just being myself; we were brought up to be kind and respectful to one another.

Sharing our hospitality was a delight. Anyone would think, seeing some of my photos that I had dated many ladies, but most were only friends and fans I had met over the years. The ladies posed in the photos as though they were dating the hottest guy in Bermuda. What a boost!

I continued entertaining at night during the peak summer months. During the day, I eventually found a job at the Bermuda Telephone Company, working in the Marketing Division. The company was situated in the city of Hamilton. This job gave me work and insurance benefits throughout the year. Having a day job was necessary, because the entertainment was seasonal. I was also paying a mortgage on the house.

Over the years, I had been financially okay from money earned from *The Variations* and Holiday Inn, so I had purchased an additional five acres of land in St. David's. Now, this had been sold, so funds could be given to my divorced wife. Although I was young at the time, I was smart enough to invest in real estate. I had taken the girls there and told them that, someday, the land would be all theirs. It had a beautiful view, over-looking the ocean.

Little did I know that divorce would destroy that dream. The girls received money from that land sale, but that was never the way I had imagined when I promised.

I began with the Bermuda Telephone Company by training in the field, installing communications, for the first year. The company had an excellent training program. I also trained in Boston for high-tech security systems, a product also offered to customers. I grasped the field of high-tech security systems and communications very quickly. Although I had no previous telephone company experience, I had good business experience and people skills.

After two years, the manager of the marketing division and I had an encounter with the chain of authority. He gave me the impression that he was rather insecure. I really liked him, but his impression of me was invalid. He must have thought I wanted his job. I was doing so well with my customers; whenever they wanted to expand their communication systems, they called and asked for me, personally. One day, I overheard a phone conversation of the manager saying to someone, "What do you want to speak to David about?" (David is the name I used in all my administration jobs. Jay is the name I used as an entertainer.) He continued, "I'm the marketing manager!" I found out later that he was talking to one of my customers.

The marketing manager oversees the work, but I felt it rather childish of him to say what he had said to my customer. I'm a person who studies for a job very thoroughly in all that I do, whether mopping floors or being a knowledgeable service advisor. I felt uneasy from that day on, despite my knowledge and the trust of my customers. I considered my options. I felt that all my expertise and certification was in hotel management. I then asked myself, "Why waste my time at the telephone company?" I needed to find a way to use my training to support my entertainment career.

I met some very important people while working in the city of Hamilton. An elderly man gave me some good advice. At the time, I was about to do my first album. He knew I was an entertainer at night, and I told him of my upcoming project. He told me. "Observe Hubert Smith;" he was the entertainer who sang the song *Bermuda Is Another World*. The song became a big hit for him in Bermuda. He was an ambassador who travelled and sang abroad to promote the island tourism. The elderly gentlemen continued, "Find out what he is doing and how he is doing it, and do it better. That goes for any business or career that you may be doing."

I embraced his advice, and I, too, became an ambassador for Bermuda. I travelled abroad to promote tourism and also recorded very popular songs. The elderly gentlemen also gave me five thousand dollars toward the album project, with no strings attached. I found out later that he owned a major portion of the city. He had been given an opportunity at the beginning of his career, so he wanted to pass on that generosity.

As time moved on, I had missed working in the hotel industry, plus it paid more. Bermuda was, and still is, one of the most expensive places in the world to live. Since things were very costly, I had to continue evenings as an entertainer to pay my increasing living expenses. I was now hungry for the hotel experience, once again.

I applied for a position as the assistant Food and Beverage Controller at the Southampton Princess Hotel. It is the largest hotel in Bermuda. Since I had all the experience and certificates, my application was successful. It included a good salary with benefits and bonuses. I was careful to negotiate free time, evenings and weekends. Work responsibilities then would have interfered with my entertainment schedule.

Later, I passed up many opportunities to be promoted to a higher position. In my experience, higher positions do not always fall in your favor. They usually entail longer hours and increased responsibility. Promotion would not be worth what it would cost me.

I began working at the hotel, starting as an assistant Food and Beverage Controller. As usual, the 'powers that be' were very cautious about hiring a Bermudian to handle the big responsibility as head of the department. I smiled to myself and thought. "I'm in; that's all that matters."

It was not long after that they found out that I was very capable, and I was promoted to head of the department. Although this was a promotion, it was still a day job. Top jobs had to be advertised annually to make way for qualified Bermudians. I was aware of this and prepared myself by being very productive at our department-head meetings with suggestions and cost-saving ideas. An example would be my investigations into dish and glass washing equipment. I could not understand why there was so much breakage of champagne glasses. They are a fragile glass, so I stood in the kitchen one night observing the cleaning procedure. I eventually found out that they were going off like pop-corn in the dish washer. The employees were sending them through in the same powerful washer as the china. I suggested, in a department-head meeting, that they install a separate glass washing machine. This turned out to be a major cost savings. I did motion studies in several other areas and discovered many other cost-saving ideas. Southampton Princess was a very large hotel, over a thousand guests served three times per day, so you can imagine how much breakage there was daily.

During the time as the head of the department, I saw clearly that Bermudians were not getting the top jobs. I couldn't really pin-point the problem. I did not know if it was race or if the 'powers that be' wanted non-Bermudians in the higher positions for other reasons. I did notice that the current staff, of about eight, in my department did not have certificates in their particular positions. They did not have experience in computer skills; they were only proof-reading common employees' coding. I changed all that immediately; I had meetings and inspired them all to take courses at the Bermuda College, just as the old Controller at the Holiday Inn had advised me many years previously. The staff embraced my advice, and they all took the courses. Within two years, they had all passed with distinction. I was so proud and happy about their accomplishments; it made headlines in the news-paper. Although I was their proctor and practical trainer, I gave all the credit to the General Manager, at the time. It made him look good, and now Bermudians in that hotel were respected for their capabilities.

The staff gave me the greatest compliment; they told me it was like coming to college everyday and not just coming to work. Now that I look back, that was my legacy. I had always trained others before moving on, Bermudians as well as nonBermudians. I was never in my life discriminatory toward anyone, except the unjust. I did not have a preference of who my staff were, or what nationality. I always encouraged anyone who was willing to learn, and assured them that I would help them to achieve their best.

I remember my first job at the Air Force Base commissary, after receiving a superior performance award. I was then promoted to a department head. It had started as simply mopping floors. When I first started mopping floors, I swung the mop side to side all the way down the aisle. I thought I had done a good job until the manager pointed out my problem. When the floor dried, it left heart shaped dirt marks all the way down the aisle on both sides. He then showed me that I needed to do both sides first before doing the center of the aisle. It was a lesson to be learned from an experienced leader. I was seventeen at the time. It showed me how a good manager helps staff. I tried to do the same throughout my career.

One day, I came to work, and a new Head Controller of Accounts had been hired. The Head of all Accounts was over my control office. He was okay to work with for awhile, but, then, the old discrimination mentality came back. Bermudians did not get the top jobs. It was 'who you knew' and 'who you had to please' in order to get the job, it seemed. Upper-level executives brought into

Bermuda usually left after a period of time, when their mission was accomplished. This new Controller decided he wanted to stay forever on the beautiful island of Bermuda. Of course, who would not want to? He made in-roads in the community by getting involved in an exclusive club and wanted to impress them.

There was a young man who was the son of an important business man who was also a Commander in the Bermuda Regiment. He was graduating from college, and a position was to be made for him. The controller told me, right to my face, that he was going to have my office report to the new, inexperienced graduate. At this time, my feelings about politics were not good. The new man was not one of the staff who had completed the hotel management courses at the Bermuda College. If the Controller had promoted one of these individuals, I would have been happy. Unfortunately, he hired the new graduate. I resented the new Controller's unjust actions. When the present staff was overlooked for promotion, it made me furious. The whole purpose of encouraging the staff to take courses and become certified was so that they could advance their careers, wages and position. In my opinion, the decision, between his style of management and mine, was easy. When I could not believe in a course of action; I did not want to be a part of their team. It seemed I always faced problems beyond my control. I found that the Bermuda Government had also sold itself out to foreign companies. Although they had policies in place to promote qualified Bermudians, most of those employees were in lower-paying jobs. Happily it has improved over the years since that time.

My entertainment career began to soar. I had now recorded an album and was very much in demand. I just wanted to perform. It was so much more satisfying for me than to deal with the cut-throat dealings going on behind the scene with hotel management. I loved the job and department that I managed personally, but I did not like the politics. The job did provide an extra income, needed because of the high cost of living in Bermuda. It also covered health insurance and social security for later on in life. Being an entertainer did not cover these expenses. This was the trap I often faced, trying to be a professional entertainer.

Fortunately, my entertainment career was soaring,,.album sales, night spots and more. The Department of Tourism was now asking for my services. It was then that I had to ask the President and General Manager of the hotel, who had to liaison with the Controller, for permission to leave my department for a few days to promote tourism abroad. Their hotel would benefit as much the other hotels. I would be a 'Song Ambassador' for Bermuda.

Looking back over the years, I was successful in all my applications, exploring and discovering opportunities all around me. To me, it was like an adventure, travelling from port to port, discovering new horizons. This was mainly because I had embraced the old Controller's advice about taking courses at the beginning of my career to become certified. I also took the time to listen to experienced leaders who had shared good advice and others who trained me in the practical field in international hotels. I had taken the advice as a gift and learned with a happy heart. I learned from a very early age from my grandfather, that it 'takes a village' to get it right. A person learns from everyone who touches his life.

ENTERTAINMENT BUSINESS

At this time in my entertainment career, I wanted the freedom to call my own shots, so this was a good opportunity to move on, once again. I was hired to travel to Montreal, Canada by the Minister of Tourism, the Honorable Mr. Colin Selly. Arriving at the Bonaventure Hotel, they checked me into a beautiful suite. I felt as though I was being treated like a king. During the evening that week, I performed for a Travel Agent Convention hosted by the Bermuda Department of Tourism. During the day, I got to see beautiful Quebec. One night when I did not have to perform, I had the opportunity to see a cabaret show with an eighteen-piece orchestra. A travel agent who had seen me perform at the convention the night before informed the band leader that I was in the audience. She must have given him a good report, because he invited me to come up on stage to sing a song. Unexpectedly, I became excited and accepted. I sang Frank Sinatra's song, *My Way*. It was a great orchestra, and the song went over very well. The promotional trip for Bermuda and I were both successful.

The following year, the Minister of Tourism hired me to travel to Vancouver, BC, again, to promote Bermuda. This time, I was checked into the top floor of the Four Seasons Hotel. Talk about being treated like a celebrity. It was hard to be humble. The bedroom was reached by a spiral staircase, from the sitting room below. The room had full-length windows from top to bottom and across the whole length of the living room. From this magnificent viewpoint, you could see the harbor with the snowy mountains in the background.

I remember sitting there, writing a post card to my mother, thanking her for the guitar she had chosen for my fifteenth birthday gift. I could not believe where that guitar had taken me, to places far beyond my imagination. I performed at many local hotel conventions; visiting corporations from many other countries came to Bermuda because of its beauty and climate. I was now in demand to put together shows with other great musicians. I was in my glory, "Jay Fox, the Wayne Newton of Bermuda." I continued performing nights in hotel night-clubs and at conventions.

It was at one of these events that an unexpected reappearance happened. Remember Donna, from my teenage days and the 'sacred cove?' Our next encounter is a Cinderella story. Fifteen years had gone since we had last seen each other; I was about to perform at a Ball Room dance in a grand hotel. I was on stage, with my back turned away from the dance floor preparing for my performance. I heard a familiar voice behind me. The voice said, "Hi, handsome." I thought for a second, "Can it be?" I turned, and I could not believe my eyes. That smile, that wonderful smile, it glowed and over-shadowed the gorgeous evening gown she was wearing. It was a formal affair; the men wore black tuxedos and the women were dressed in beautiful evening gowns. However, she looked special. The glow on her face was indescribable. I had not seen her in over 15 years or more. She had matured into a beautiful woman. What a wonderful surprise. I melted, all over again. I don't remember what happened after we talked for a while, but she disappeared. I just know I could not find the 'missing slipper.' Why we had been so protective of each other, I don't know. I do know that no one will ever call us selfish. We each made a lot of sacrifices not to hurt others. Again, I did not see her for many years that followed. Through that meeting, I saw a very strong, confident woman. Two people had loved each other in a very special way, the way God loved us, when He protected us in that sandy 'sacred cove.' This story continues as an incredible discovery in a later chapter of this book.

I spent days working on a diving boat named the Ovation. Boy! How great was that, Jay Fox in Jimmy Buffet style? All I had to do was play my guitar, sing songs on an island cruise and go snorkeling all day. This was wonderful, but rum swizzles and hot sun can get to you after awhile. It was fun, but I was too tired from the salty air and tropical drinks to perform my shows later that night.

One full season I was booked at two locations in one night. I did a show at a major hotel, called "Big Night Out" starring Scott McKay, Paddy Parnell, the Sheila Holt dancers and myself with Kae's Show-band. It was a slick, non-stop revue of comedy, magic, music and dance. I started at 8 PM at the world-famous Henry VIII pub and restaurant. At this location I performed a Jimmy Buffet-style act. Then, I left to go perform an hour in the style of Frank Sinatra at the "Big Night Out" show. While traveling in the car, I changed from a Hawaiian shirt into a tux.

Mike Bishop with his Saturday night show guests, Sheila Holt Dancers and Jay Fox

'Jay Fox' Starring in 'The Big Night Out'

One evening, I arrived, and the Sheila Holt Dancers were all seated in a row, still putting on their makeup. As I approached the dressing room, Paddy Parnell was ahead of me and had just finished a Phyllis Diller comedy act. She had rushed in, thrown her wig on a chair, put on another wig and headed back on stage to complete the second part of the act. At that moment, I stood there in my tux waiting for the announcer to introduce me. I looked at the girls and

95

then looked at the wig, and then said, "Should I? Should I?" They immediately knew what I meant. They cheered me on..."Yes! Yes!" was their enthusiastic reply. I put on the blonde, Phyllis Diller wig and entered the stage. The performers Scott McKay and Paddy were still on stage. I was to join them for part-two of the act. As soon as they saw me, they stood there in total shock. They were lost for words. The audience, who knew me, thought it was hilarious and squalled with laughter. However, Scott was the producer. After our performance, back stage, he jumped right onto me. He said, "Don't ever do that again." He was very upset. The cast then went to the lobby to meet the audience, as we did after every performance. Many from the audience stopped and shook my hand and said how much they had enjoyed that part of the show. The producer saw how the people were gathering around me, praising the prank. They were giving me so much attention that Scott finally came over, apologized for his outburst and said, "It was a great spontaneous move.

I continued to bury myself in my work and doing the thing which I loved the most, being an entertainer. I was invited, as a special guest, to sing on the Mike Bishop Show. The Sheila Holt Dancers joined me during the performance. It was a local production, similar to the David Letterman Show. On one occasion, Mike Bishop had his TV Show on a cruise ship while it was in port, and I was a special guest. As time progressed, I produced my own television show. It was a special half-hour show for heritage month celebration for Bermuda. I had special guests, local recording artists *Tony and Owen*. They had recently released a new single called *Last Night I Fell in Love.*

Entertaining was instilled in my blood like an addiction. The entertainment business was not only financially lucrative; it was my creative outlet in life. My heart and soul were poured out into writing songs and being an entertainer. Over the years, my fans encouraged me to record my original songs. Year after year, as they returned to the island for vacations, they searched the hotels to find my entertaining schedule.

The number of fans had grown tremendously; they asked immediately, had I recorded more of my original songs or- when would I record again? I promised them that every penny I made in the entertainment business I would save to record another album. I kept my promise that year and prepared to record my fourth album in the United States at Suma Recording Studio in Cleveland, Ohio. In preparation, I needed to arrange to have a photo shoot for an album cover. I was beginning to show a little gray hair that was not evenly distributed. It was rather patchy-looking, so before the photo session, I made an appointment to have my hair dyed.

Not knowing the salon procedure, I asked the hair stylist to dip a comb in some dark dye and comb it through my hair. She, of course, had to do it the 'correct way.' To my dismay, my hair color came out purple! The mixture had not turned out the way she expected. I shouted, "Oh God! What have you done?" She panicked, and was very sorry for the results. She began to wash it out with another substance, which was bleach. My scalp began to burn, tremendously. I was going crazy, thinking my hair would all fall out. She dyed it again, but it turned out jet black. I was extremely upset and vowed I would never dye my hair again. I had to live with the final results. The photo came out okay; it became the cover on *Island of Paradise.*

While at Suma, I had several experiences, things I never could have expected. Suma's recording package had accommodations included. I checked into one of their log cabins on the premises, and when I entered the room, a bat flew right at me and almost frightened me to death. I had never seen a live bat in my life. We don't have them in Bermuda. The next day, I had a tough session in the studio, nervousness, I guess. I took a break and decided to take a walk outside. As I was walking, I reached down to pick up a dark stick lying on the ground. What I thought was a stick quickly slithered away. I ran back into the studio screaming, "Snake, snake; there's a snake out there in the grass." The owners and studio musicians laughed, helplessly. I found out, after the laughter, that it was only a harmless, black garden snake. Again, I had never seen a snake in my life. We don't have them in Bermuda, either. I was learning many unexpected things. For a few days I was a nervous wreck. During this trip, I completed half of the recording project. A few months later, I returned to Suma Recording Studio, in the middle of winter, to finish the album, and I experienced another first. While driving to Suma, a snow storm came off Lake Erie, and I encountered a white-out. Again, there is no snow in Bermuda. It snowed so hard that day, the road disappeared. I had no idea where to go. Finally, an eighteen wheeler plowed through and left tracks. I followed it to the nearest exit. The recording studio had many famous artists record there. It was no 'corner shop.' *Wild Cherry* recorded an album there. I was in professional hands. The album project turned out great, in spite of the educational encounters I had had with new and strange animals and weather.

When I returned home from the United States, I went immediately to the radio station to release a single from my new album. The song was *Crystal Waters*. On the island of Bermuda, it was a hit. It continued to play on the radio very often. Unfortunately, the day I released the album, I had no one else with whom to celebrate this great accomplishment. I was so excited while driving along the highway listening to my new song. The DJ had just announced, "Hi folks; here's Jay Fox's latest release, hot off the press, *Crystal Waters*. I began shouting, "I did it! I did it!" Since I was alone, I decided to go into the city of Hamilton. I sat outside on the terrace of a restaurant above Front Street to savor the moment. The restaurant was overlooking the harbor. It was a spectacular view, similar to the scene when the sun was sparkling like diamonds on the water which had inspired me to write the song. While I was sitting out on the terrace, a lady came out and introduced herself. Her name was Catherine. She had recognized me. After my divorce, I had no one to go home to. It seemed, after my children were taken away from me, I went into a careless state. I just buried myself in my music. I went to disco clubs and danced the night away after performing. The most popular night spot after hours was the Little Venice Disco Club. It was there that I'm sure she had seen me. During our conversation, we found that we had many similarities. She had sung in a band called *Day by Day* with a good friend of mine, who, shockingly, was murdered as he worked late one night as manager in a grocery store. The young man and I had served in the Bermuda Regiment. We were both Corporals and had served a few years together before he was killed. He played trumpet in her band. His name was Mark Doe. She told me the names of her brother and father. Her brother, Andrew, was a popular keyboard player in the group called *Sharks*. Her father, Jimmy, was a well-known classical pianist. I knew them well because of their popularity. They both performed throughout the island. She told me she was once married and had a daughter named Kimberly. From that moment on, we shared so much in common that we spent a lot of time together. Catherine began to travel with me to my performances. She was a great singer, herself. Her style was somewhat of a combination of Carly Simon, Carol King and Bette Midler. With her talented singing ability, every now and then, I invited her to come up on stage to do a duet with me. The audience loved the special treat of hearing her sing with me.

Jay Fox, new album, *Signature* featuring six of his own compositions; *Think of Me There, Jenny, Silently, Crystal Waters, Suzanne* and *Bermuda Brings Back Such - Memories.*

Included on the album are a few of the island's most popular songs; *Bermuda is Another World, Today, This Is Bermuda,* and, his personal favorite, *Precious & Few.*

Jay has performed in every major Hotel and Cottage Colony, in Bermuda: Holiday Inn, Elbow Beach Hotel, Sonesta Beach Hotel, Southampton Princess, The Reefs Hotel, Pink Beach Hotel, Cambridge Beaches and Pompano Beach Hotel and Cottage Colony.

Catherine loved horses and competed often at dressage events. I had attended these events long before I met her. I loved to watch but never intended to ride a horse, myself.

We continued to date for several months. Our relationship began to grow, and it seemed we were never apart. We even performed in a popular musical called *Joseph and the Amazing Technicolor Dream Coat*.

On December 5th 1982, Catherine and I got married. We had a beautiful daughter and named her Jacqueline. Her interest, from the very beginning of her journey in life, was fashion and the Arts. She loved getting into her mom's clothing and dressing up, from a very early age, including makeup and jewelry. When it came to the Arts, Jacqueline frequently put on theatrical shows for the family, especially at Christmas. She often was found in my home recording studio, practicing musicals from movies. She learned all the songs from the movie Beaches and performed them incredibly. At age eleven, she performed the songs at a concert in a very large building in the city of Hamilton, Bermuda. School children from all over the island attended. It was a special event, put on by the Government, for the children of Bermuda. Her class-mates did not know that Jacqueline sang. Of course, she sang for fun with her friends, but this performance had been presented very professionally. As soon as she came off the stage, her fellow students and students from other schools flocked around her. Instant fame frightened her. It took her many years to perform in front of people again.

THE TRIP BACK TO ENGLAND

Eleven years had passed since finding my father. We had written back and forth, sharing phone calls, letters, photos and memories. A void in my life had been filled. He was now, not just a wonderful memory my mother shared, but a reality of a loving father I had finally gotten to know, in person. I discovered that he was real and why my mother loved him so. We had the same churning, turning, roiling longings, the tide of the same blood running through both of our veins. I was a clone-copy of him in looks and in the things we loved, including music. We sang the same songs, even though we were years apart. He sang those great old songs by Perry Como, And, *I Love Her So* and Jim Reeves, *He'll Have To Go*. In years that followed, he sang songs from John Denver and Neil Diamond, some of my favorite artists, as well as others I often sang. I had his talent running through my veins. Added to that talent, I had my mother's charm and magnetism. Children and adults loved her and called her 'Nana.' She was so kind, gentle, patient and caring. I finally understood why she had remained so faithful to one person.

For years, I had observed women in St. David's, who had several children from different fathers. Many of the children grew up not knowing their fathers. This was the down side of the influx of the American and British military, beginning in the late 1940's. It continued for 30 or more years, men promising to return but never fulfilling that promise for one reason or another. For years, I felt that I was just another statistic. I was just another fatherless child.

I had gravitated toward the Priest of the church I attended in those early years. I guess that's why I loved being a choir and altar boy. The Priest loved the children of St. David's. He was surrounded by hundreds over the years. My mother loved me dearly, but the Priest, Rev. Sidney C. Little, was a fatherly image for me and many other children. He ministered at the 'Chapel of Ease' in St. David's, in the 50s and 60s. Rev. Little was so loved by the children. He made us feel special, like we were his own children. There were eleven boys in his Vacation Bible School group who later became choir and altar boys, in their teens. Most of us in the photo are sitting on the step in a row and some others are standing in the middle. I, eventually, became a youth leader until I was eighteen.

Chapel of Ease, St. David's, Rev. Sidney C. Little is top center, surrounded by children and the adult leaders of Vacation Bible School.

This love is now passed on as I carry out the tradition of teaching Vacation Bible School and have become very involved in my local church.

In 1989, my father was diagnosed with cancer; it did not regress as some have experienced. I rushed to his bedside, thousands of miles from Bermuda, traveling again that long journey to the little village in Hadfield, England. Along with me on the journey were my wife, Catherine, and my youngest daughter, Jacqueline. After a few days, he showed me where the cancer had developed. As he was lying there in our last quiet moments together, he told me to take care of my mother; she is a wonderful person. As I held his hand, he lost the battle to that horrible disease, cancer. My rediscovered father was gone.

Before I returned to Bermuda, Pat handed me a folder of songs my father had sung. They were all hand-written in print, the way I prepare my songs. Many of the songs were those I had already, in my folder at home, which I had printed to learn in my shows as an entertainer. I felt that we were one, in mind, body and spirit. After a few days, Catherine and I, with little Jacqueline left on that long journey back home to Bermuda. I had finally gotten to know my father before I lost him and had discovered, and come to know, brother, sisters and a new mother. I understood, at this time in my life, how finding my father after not knowing him for the first 28 years and his sudden death after only 11 years of contact had affected me. I needed to spend more time with my wife and children, other than just providing for them. Family had become important to me.

During those early years of having Julie and Rebecca separated from me and taken across to the United States, I had really needed to feel their presence. They had finally moved to the East Coast, so I decided to purchase a time share in Florida. I figured having a time share gave me a guaranteed vacation time, no matter how things got, financially. In Orlando, I visited them more often. We had wonderful times together. I spoiled them each year to make up for the past when I could not see them. Each year I took them to Disney World. One year there, I took the girls to a hair salon. When they came out, they looked beautiful. Returning to the hotel, they both jumped in the pool. I could not believe what had just happened. Then I thought, "Who cares that their hair has just been done." It was wonderful to see the joy on their face; Hairdos were not nearly as important to me as their happiness.

Having everyone in my life nearby, it seemed I had everything that I needed; however, something very important was missing in my life...God.

THE REVELATION

Looking back over the years before I turned forty, I realized that I had poured my entire life into my hotel career and entertaining business. I then asked the question, "Who was watching over me, and helping my mom, a single mother with a young child? Who was responsible for my successful business and entertainment careers as well as my close and loving family?" A chill came over me...I knew then, my Heavenly Father was watching over us, both then and now.

When all these feelings came to a head, I drove down the beautiful south shore of Bermuda, overlooking the ocean and breathing in its beauty. I sat, looking out at the ocean, pondering all that had happened in my lifetime, the successes and adversities. I had allowed the behavior of people to turn me away from God. Because of those stormy experiences in churches and my previous marriage, I had just buried myself in work and had left the church completely. Had God given up on me? I knew he had not.

One day, my revelation was confirmed. My mother in-law told me that the Church of the Nazarene congregation where she attended was praying for me. Their prayer was for me to attend their service. She asked if I could sing at a luncheon they were having at their family center. At first, I did not know how to respond. I said to myself, "What will I sing?" I felt that show business tunes would not be appropriate in a church fellowship gathering. Then a 'Small Voice' inside my head said, "Remember the songs I inspired you to write when you were close by my side?"

There were days, before I left the church, when I studied the Bible, often. God had touched me in many ways. Many times I had written how He had changed my life. During that time, I had written a song called Change in Me.

> *Change in my heart, there's a change I can't describe.*
> *Joy in my soul, there's a change.*
> *It happened kind of sudden, I cast away my pride.*
> *I looked for change to come.*
> *I asked God to guide me, through all the years to*
> *come, To take my hand and lead, me on*

I had written another song called *I Came to Find My Jesus,* the song I sang at the Seventh Day Adventist revival with Charles Brookes as the speaker back in the late seventies. This was the song which had lifted the elderly lady's spirit. The song is about a young man in search of this precious, loving Jesus everyone was talking about. The young man searched hills and valleys. Later, he knelt to pray in an open field.

> *Oh, tell me; where I can find him, this precious*
> *loving Jesus?*
> *Oh, why am I so blind?*

At that moment, Jesus revealed Himself, in the young man's vision, kneeling right next to him. Jesus had been with him all along, just waiting for him to ask. Another time, I had composed a song called Victory Feelings. It's a story of victory, finding Jesus, telling everyone to trust in Him through all the storms in our lives.

"Victory feelings we have in thee, crossing our lives through history; with God as our Master and God as our friend."

There were many other inspirational songs I had written...later shelving them, thinking no one would be interested in them. I had not done anything with them, because the churches at that time were very traditional.

The songs I had written were in the style of the artists I had grown up with in the 70's and in the style I would have played in the band. The traditionalists in the church called them too secular. If they had listened to the words and not just the music, they would have understood and received a blessing; as the elderly lady had done. God was in every loving stanza. I did not know, at the time when I wrote them, that God was inspiring me to share those lyrics and encouraging me to not be discouraged by the people who rejected the style, but I was now beginning to figure it out.

At that very moment, having that conversation with my mother in-law, when she asked me to sing, I knew that God was speaking to me through her. I could hear God saying,

"I'm going to use your gift of singing to further my Kingdom."

For many years, I had blamed God for the churches' congregations, their mistakes and narrow minds and stayed away from them. I, now, found myself back in the fold where God wanted me to be. The prodigal son had returned.

For the first time, I realized that God had been right beside me all along and was now leading me into a career of gospel singing, in my style. I took a song like *How Great Thou Art,* a song they were familiar with. I added a little 'sweetener' with it as we call it in the music business. The traditional way to sing the song would be just a piano accompaniment and the congregation's voices, which was wonderful most of the time. However, I was of a new generation. I added drums, guitar and electronic string instruments...a full orchestra sound. It was a rich, full sound, and the congregation really responded. I found myself being loved for who I was and for the talent God had given rather than adulated as one of many popular entertainment 'Stars.'

I sang the songs God had given me that day, and everyone expressed how blessed they felt through the message in my songs. God was singing through my music, and people were hearing His voice.

During that year, 1990, I began attending that Church of the Nazarene. After getting involved with the music program and later having private studies with the pastor for about a year, I got baptized, in 1991. I wanted a fresh, cleansing start. I vowed, "Never will I turn away from God." I began studying with the pastor and having a new regeneration experience. During this period, my only son, Cameron, was born, January 5th, 1990. I wanted him to have a good foundation, as I had had. I now wanted all my children to know God and to know that Jesus loves them, no matter whom they are or what they have done. I knew that, when they had learned to trust and believe in Him, and if all else fails, He would always be there for them. It amazed me that from that moment of focusing on God, how He opened doors and things began to change for me.

My prayer, as I tell you this, is not to condemn others for what they do or say but to show what God can do in your life when you focus on Him. I've learned not to internalize what others do or say; that, sometimes, can destroy a relationship with God. As we grow and have a stronger relationship with God, He allows us to be filled with the Holy Spirit, which gives us understanding of past circumstances. He empowers us to forgive. Forgiveness is thoughtfulness of the other person's perspective. Did he or she mean to be unkind because they simply were misunderstood? We can learn a lot when we think positive. If a person is impolite and cross-tempered, maybe he or she is worried or in pain. Maybe he or she has been misunderstood or been misinformed about something we have said or done. Forgiveness is easier if we try to understand, before we allow ourselves to condemn.

"A man's wisdom gives him patience; it is to his glory to overlook an offense" (Proverbs 19:11). It is said, "No attitude is godlier than to forgive or to overlook a wrong." "Love keeps no records of wrong" (1 Corinthians 13:5)

The Holy Spirit enables us to respond with His love when we ask, "God, I can't do it myself, do something for me, help me to forgive." With joy and relief you will feel no bitterness toward that person. Thank the Lord, for His grace, and that He'll always be available for those who need understanding.

"See to it that no one misses the grace of God and that no bitter root grows up to cause trouble and defile many" (Hebrews 12:15).

I do not ask anyone to question his doctrines or beliefs, but I do suggest that all should focus on Jesus Christ and His death on the Cross, and ask God in prayer, for a greater understanding of the Gospel. Real love does not see color, rich or poor. God's love commands us to believe on the name of Jesus Christ and to love one another. (1 John 3:23) I am grateful that God took the hurt and resentment from my heart and allowed me to forgive.

DECLINE IN THE
BERMUDA ECONOMY

After marrying Catherine, having Jacqueline and then Cameron, things were going well for me. However, my mother had gotten very ill, once more. Her asthma had taken a toll on her. She was admitted to the hospital. At this point, Catherine and I decided that she should move in with us. We made arrangements to sell the house and search for a larger one. We found a large house with an adjacent, little cottage. My mother was relocated, after coming out of hospital, into this little cottage. She loved it! She was very near the grandchildren. Jacqueline would always be found walking across the lawn with her blanket to snuggle up with her 'Nana.' The grandchildren would always find comfort and warmth with her.

The estate also had an adjacent garage which I converted into a recording studio. It was the perfect solution to our problem. Taking on this additional expense meant that I would have to supplement our income. Once again, I entered into the hotel management job market.

The Elbow Beach Hotel, on the beautiful south shore of Bermuda, needed a Purchasing Director. The Director of Human Resource knew of my past experience in Purchasing at the Holiday Inn. He and I had worked together, previously. He was one of the staff members I had trained to take over my position as Food and Beverage Controller, years ago. He had advanced in his career. He knew of my continued experience in other major hotels. Because of this, he persuaded me to join the Elbow Beach Hotel Management Team.

After working there for a few years, things were going very well. Then the storms of life hit once more. During the 1990's, the hotels on the island and everywhere experienced a low occupancy due to lack of tourism. People didn't have the money to travel. In October, of 1991, my position was made redundant. It left me in shock because, within a few years, I had saved the hotel thousands of dollars in purchasing supplies. With my professional skills, I had been able to save money for the hotel due to the poor management of the previous Purchasing Director compared to my system of careful observation and thoughtful management. They had to eliminate many other positions, and, because they reduced executive positions along with other staff workers positions, they thought they would not have repercussions from the Workers Union or accusations of discrimination.

The President of the Union was very powerful in Bermuda. He could cripple the island in many areas of the industry by calling strikes. Over the years, there had been many strikes and walk-outs due to demands for wage increases or staff grievances. However, this was a different situation; the world economies were all affected in some way or another. During that time, Iraq invaded Kuwait, and when the United States intervened, travel literally stopped. People were afraid to travel because of the threat of terrorism. Several planes had been brought down, internationally. Flying anywhere seemed to be a big risk. It was now almost impossible to get jobs in the hotel industry. All the hotels had suffered from the low occupancy situation. I was, at the time, a very highly-paid executive. It had included bonus pay for an outstanding performance, and my performance had been outstanding. Being laid off made me feel like a ship let loose to drift to an unknown destination. It was a horrible feeling like being tossed in a storm totally out of control, at the mercy of the surging water.

After the decline in the hotel industry, I was forced to make a major career change once again. For five years following that involuntary career change, I found myself floating in job areas that I did not fully enjoy. There was a short time when I enjoyed being Territory Manager for Proctor and Gamble. I had to fly to Cincinnati, Ohio to be interviewed for the job and was, once again, successful in the application. BGA Group of Companies was a large distribution firm that handled P&G supplies on the island. Soon, they also found themselves in a financial downslide due to the decline in the economy.

The hotel industry lay-offs naturally affected the entertainment business, where I was highly in demand. Being an entertainer and also a hotel executive had been very lucrative for me. When all this was gone, I was unable to afford the mortgage on my home. My job search and financial problems now became a major concern. Things had been going very well before the economy took a nose dive. I had found peace with God. It was during this time of spiritual regeneration that I used the talent God had given me. I began to sing in the church and do gospel concerts throughout the island. One week, when I was about to perform a benefit concert for the handicapped, I was also in the recording studio doing a new gospel CD of the songs I had written. An idea came to me to release a single from the CD to promote the concert. I did this and ordered four CDs. Two were sent to two local radio stations, and one was sent to Dominion Marketing, a music promoter in Nashville. The last of the four CDs I kept as a memento. The concert was received very well. During this gospel music ministry, I was blessed to share it with Song Evangelist, Mark Norman Murphy; he had recently recorded his song *Forgiven* composed in 1990. Joining us also was his good friend Rio Clemente, on piano.

Later, my first gospel CD was completed; myself and Rev. Manuel J. Chavier, Jr., Pastor of the Church of the Nazarene in

Bermuda, arrived at the Church of the Nazarene District Assembly, held in New Bedford, New England. The year was 1996. I was invited to travel from Bermuda to sing and begin my Song Evangelist Ministry. A year went by, and as I was lying in my bed studying the Bible, the phone rang. I answered; the caller identified himself as Dan "Christian" Beaver, from Christian Galleria Marketing in Nashville. After the introduction, he said that he liked the CD, and it had great potential. He said he was no longer with Dominion Marketing and had opened his own music promotion company. He wanted to know if I'd like to come to Nashville, Tennessee to promote my latest gospel CD throughout the United States. My dream had always been to be internationally known as a songwriter, but I never realized it would be in gospel music.

The opportunity had arisen, so I decided to follow up on his proposal. It coincided with the time we had to use our vacation week in Orlando. I called the time share management (RCI) and asked if we could transfer our time share vacation to Tennessee. They said it would be no problem. We made arrangements to stay in Fairfield Glade, an hour or more east of Nashville. Catherine and I traveled to Nashville, Tennessee to meet with the promoter. The promoter showed us a very viable plan, and the contract was signed.

He advised us to purchase a home in Tennessee, which could be used as a home base. While vacationing in Fairfield Glade, we scouted around the area of Crossville. It was centrally located. I did not want to live in a city like Nashville. We did find a suitable place.

Catherine was, of course, interested in equestrian competitions. She found a retired policeman and his wife who had a small equestrian facility. After discussing her experience as an equestrian trainer, they offered her a job, if we were to make the final step to move to Tennessee. She also found an equestrian club in Knoxville she planned to join. All the ducks were in line. All we had to do was to go home and wait for immigration approval. Catherine and I returned to Bermuda to start processing the immigration papers.

Back at home, I pondered all that I would be leaving behind, especially my boats. One day I got the most unusual news; a wind storm had sunk my 20' Sea Ray, with a brand new 150 mercury outboard motor. It was the only one in the marina that sank, because of a direct hit on it from a freak water spout. It had been under water for three days before someone notified me. I was shocked. The motor was completely destroyed. The seats also were destroyed. Everything in the boat was ruined except the boat itself. I did not have it insured, because I knew I was going to have to sell it. I hated to make these sacrifices. It was one of the things that had been holding me back from moving. I sold what was left of the Sea Ray. My next door neighbor had twin boys. He was such a great guy, so I gave him the Sunfish sailboat as a gift for his sons. That tie was now cut as well.

While we were waiting for Immigration's decision, Catherine received a phone call from the retired policeman who owned the equestrian facility in Crossville. He said his wife had left him. He asked Catherine if she would consider coming to Tennessee now. She would be his trainer. He had several students who were left without anyone to guide them. He also had other horses in training. Catherine accepted his offer.

We listed our house with a realtor. He knew it was a steal price, to sell it quickly. Without a blink of the eye, he purchased the house, himself. We made double what we had paid for it, but I considered it to be worth more. The economy being the way it was, I took the offer. We were free to go, and everything was in order; we thought.

My wife and I and our two children came to the United States, the land of dreams...so they say. As it turned out, the promoter's immigration application for me and my family was rejected. They actually told him that I was not considered a 'star', yet, and proof of concert sales would have to be presented as evidence. The promoter offered me an opportunity to manage his retreat hotel in Branson until the concerts materialized. This information was also included in the same application. Immigration must have not even considered my hotel qualifications.

By this time, I had already sold my home in Bermuda and had moved to Tennessee. With all the qualifications I had, compared to the general applicants, I believed that God had opened this door, so I took this step of faith. I invested thousands of dollars from the sale of our home in Bermuda and an inheritance from our parents, into the purchase of a home, vehicles and living expenses to manage in Crossville, Tennessee until approval was given. Our time granted in the United States was three to six months, and when we finally got the answer from the Immigration Office, this period had passed. We approached Senator Van Hilary's office in Crossville, to ask for advice on what to do. They told us at Van Hilary's office not to worry; they get bus loads of Mexican immigrants here, very often. Catherine and I stood there absolutely puzzled. What was that comment supposed to mean? What were we expected to do? The presence of Mexican immigrants was no surprise to us, because we had seen them around the area, but we weren't 'wetbacks'. This was very upsetting to us in our situation, because we were from Bermuda, a British Colony, and were both skilled professionals. We did not want to be considered illegal immigrants. This was very stressful. We didn't know what to do, but God, once again, opened a door.

Once we had arrived in Tennessee and purchased a home, I wanted to set a strong spiritual foundation for the family. We attended a Nazarene church near our home. Once again in my life, I got very involved in the church. I volunteered as Minister of Music. I, eventually, taught all phases of Sunday school, from youth to adults. I served on the church board, and one thing led to another. It was suggested that I enroll in Ministerial Studies. It was now twenty-seven years since I had heard those same words at Holiday Inn, "Enroll in studies." It was important for me to study and improve myself in ministry. Since I had been studying Theology and Ministry to become certified, I re-applied, including my family, for our Adjustment of Immigration Status, through our local church. Approval to proceed was given by Immigration. We learned later, from our lawyer in Nashville, that Britain and its Territory Colonies have a treaty for so many people each year to be allowed immigration. We qualified. Catherine and I finally received authorization from Immigration to work. As I write this story, my family and I are waiting for Adjustment of Status to be considered. The case is now pending, in our lawyer's hands, to rectify our situation. This is just another storm in life we face and as complicated as one can possibly imagine.

LIFE ON THE FARM

While waiting for things to develop with Immigration, we settled into the home and 30 acres we had purchased. Catherine helped the policeman to get reorganized at his facility. Later, she and I decided to develop our own equestrian facility to board and train competitive horses. This involved training both the rider and horse in the art of dressage. She concentrated on the training, and I concentrated on maintaining the property. It was a partnership we both enjoyed in the beginning.

I had been an executive and famous entertainer. The experience on the farm humbled me, yet it was one of the most incredible experiences of my life. Our day began with taking care of horses, mucking out stalls and maintaining our equestrian facility, cutting the fields, lifting hundreds of bales of hay and storing them for the winter. Catherine continued, after the morning work, training riders. I continued, after the morning work, in the music studio. It was physically and mentally challenging.

Jacqueline had attended Bermuda High School for girls. She now attended school at Cumberland County High School. She continued her love of the Arts, among other academic subjects. She and a friend from school (Steven) put on shows for us in the private setting of our 30 acre farm. Although Jacqueline loved the Arts, she never pursued it professionally. She continued to be shy in front of audiences. As time progressed, Jacqueline got engaged and eventually married her high school sweetheart.

Cameron, my son, was enrolled at North Cumberland Elementary School. Later, he attended Stone Memorial High School. He finished an exciting season of basketball with his team, the Panthers. As the year continued, the Track & Field coach found the team short a high jumper. Cameron, with his gravity-defying dunking skills in basketball, had thrilled his fans, so he was invited to try out for the track team. Little did he know a star high jumper would be born! To his and his coach's surprise, he ended the season at the State High Jump Championships.

Though a grueling competition, Cameron hung in there until the last competitive jump. The moment became very tense; the next to last jumper went before him and cleared the height of 6'4". Cameron then ran for his ascent. He cleared the same height. The bar was raised to 6'6". The competitor went once again; however, this time he pushed the bar over onto the mattress. It was now Cameron's turn; he maneuvered back and forth then began his approach toward the high cross bar. It was a tense moment for everyone watching. Cameron soared over the bar and won the State High Jump Championship. There was so much jubilation from everyone. During all the excitement, the bar was raised to 6'8". Although he had won the championship, he thought he would try again. He missed the jump, but vowed that he would achieve it next year.

The *Panthers* won their first District AA Basketball Championship in 2008. Although Cameron was not known for high scoring in the games, he was exciting to watch. Whenever he had the ball, everyone who knew him knew something special was about to happen. He was the 'Magic Johnson' (L.A. Lakers) or 'Steve Nash' (Phoenix Suns) of the team. He passed to his team players with such finesse and quickness that his team members were able to finish and score points. He was an effective support rather than a showy star.

During the opening seconds of the Championship game, Cameron drove in from the back door with a gravity-defying dunk. It set the tone for the game. His team members played their best performance of the season. Cameron ended the game with the last shot at the Free-throw line.

After basketball season, Cameron began Track & Field once again. He soon found himself in the State High Jump Championship. This time, it came down to the last competitor, once again. The height was raised to 6'6." Cameron led with the first attempt. He cleared the cross bar successfully. The competitor then approached the high bar. He, too, cleared the bar. The bar was then raised to 6'8". Cameron maneuvered back and forth as he had done the previous year. He ran, and with that spring in his legs, he flew over the bar. The competitor went again, and this time, with a tiny brush of wind from his body, the bar slowly rolled off and fell to the mattress. Cameron, once again, had won the State High Jump Championship.

For me and his coaches, it could not have been more of a proud moment. I gave Cameron the nickname 'FLY.' The school arranged a parade through Main Street, escorted by police.

It was a great achievement for the county. He was the first to ever win a State Championship. To top that, he did it two years in a row. He will be in sports history for Cumberland County. Cameron was awarded a scholarship to attend Rend Lake College, Ina, Illinois. He is now jumping consistently, hovering around seven feet. All of Cameron's high school basketball fans thought he would get a basketball scholarship, and so did he. But, he got a scholarship in Track and Field. We never know what God has in store for us.

My children have made me extremely proud over the years. They have been truly blessed by God. Julie, after graduating from high school in the United States, returned home to Bermuda to live with me. It was a joy to have her with me again. Sadly, Rebecca did not return with her. Julie attended the Nazarene church I had joined, along with the family. Eventually, she met Ernest

Peets who had just returned from a business college in the United States. He also attended the Bermuda Church of the Nazarene. He later, was called to be a preacher. They got engaged and both attended Eastern Nazarene College in Boston, Ma. He graduated with a Master of Divinity. Julie graduated with a degree in Child Development. They got married and moved back to Bermuda. Ernest and Julie have two girls and a boy. They both are now ministering in the Bermuda Church of the Nazarene.

Rebecca continues to live in Florida and has her own hair Salon. She is married to Ben Graves, who is a relief coordinator for storm disasters. Rebecca gave me my first grandson, Mycah. She also has a step daughter named Samantha, from Ben's first marriage. Mycah is a great guitar player like his grandfather and a champion swimmer.

The Graves Family
Samantha, Mycah, Ben and my daughter Rebecca Kimberly,
Catherine's daughter from her previous marriage, remained
in Bermuda. She is in banking and is married to Joey
Martins. They have two children, Ashley and Thomas.

The Martins
Kimberly (Step daughter), Joey, Ashley and Thomas

Jay's children
Top: Julie, Middle: Jacqueline and Rebecca,
Bottom: Cameron

REFLECTIONS

I had evolved from an executive and famous entertainer in my homeland, Bermuda, to a hard-working man running a farm with my wife. I found time to travel the country doing Gospel Concerts, Revivals and Camp Meetings on weekends as a Song Evangelist. My ministry has included many positive relationships with well-known evangelists such as Bob Hoots, Nelson Purdue, Richard Reed and others. Most of the concert earnings were benefits to help others in need. Our income depended on the savings we had transferred from Bermuda.

Although we enjoyed many parts of our lives on the farm, many other parts were heart breaking. Catherine and I had many disagreements about how I managed the horses compared to her opinion based upon her skills as an equestrian handler. I was not very good at it, and I had to learn. Other disagreements were about financial problems, regarding our depleted of savings verses expenses. It became a financial strain. Like most people who have to take from their life savings and use it during financial struggles, we had to stretch our inheritance funds in order to survive. When things got stressful like that, it was our love for each other that got us through all of it.

The good times on the farm were going out in the field and looking back at the beautifully-landscaped pastures. Catherine and I worked very hard each day to keep it in good shape. Jacqueline and Cameron asked their friends to come to the farm and help gather the freshly-cut hay during the summer months to store it up for the winter; their help really made a difference in getting a difficult job done.

Watching the beautiful horses out in the field was a sight to see. At feeding time, I gave a loud whistle, and the horses came running to the gate.

There were many times I went out in the middle of the field and sat on a flat stone. In that quiet moment, I took time in prayer, thanking God for all he had provided us. My Song Evangelist work was not a financial success since I donated most of that money. My peace of mind was spiritual success. I sold CDs here and there and was given a love offering once in awhile. It was only a fraction of what I had earned during the last 30 years as an entertainer and hotel executive, but I was doing what I felt was right.

My goal is to allow Catherine to achieve her goals. In supporting Catherine to reach her goals, we all succeed. I now know that she is a gift from God. She is forgiving and the hardest-working person I've ever met in my life. For me, life was all about my wife and my children. I did not want my disappointments to come between my family and me. They are the greatest joy in my life that God has given.

When Immigration first disapproved my application, naturally, I was disappointed and faced another stormy period in my life. My family and I have had to wait so long for immigration approval that it felt as though we were trapped and could not move or travel to our homeland because of their instructions.

Volunteering my services at revivals as a Song Evangelist and playing benefits around the community kept me from further discouragement. There was a great satisfaction serving the community. One year I put together a group of gospel singers to raise funds to benefit Battered Women, Inc. which is based in Cumberland County, Tennessee. The organization serves several other Counties and provides a 24 hour crisis line and emergency shelter for women and their children. The group offers crisis intervention and counseling, advocacy in the court system, referrals, and emergency financial assistance. One benefit led to another of community in need. I attended services on a regular basis and remained very involved in the ministry. I was able to remain positive and to trust in God that things will be okay.

The humility of the experience of being patient and waiting gave me time to evaluate myself. I developed a web-site, hosted by Soundclick.com, to let people know of my new CDs and latest compositions. The site is a complete listing of all the CDs I have produced over the years. You can also click on a song and hear it before purchasing it. It kept fans informed of my upcoming concerts posted and the responses from previous concerts. The web-site provided photographs, song lyrics and stories of what had inspired me to write each song. The web-site became very effective. I had an inquirer on the fan page who wanted to purchase my CDs. The inquirer became an incredible discovery. The photo of the person on the site was very small. I did not recognize the photo or the surname. I wrote back in curiosity as to how much she knew about my music. As a potential customer, I wanted to be sure that she knew a little about it, so she would be pleased after purchasing it. She replied on my website, saying she had known me for many years and had heard me play the guitar and sing. She, then, gave her address, where I had to send my CD. Our tweeting, back and forth, made me more curious to know where she had seen me perform. My son happened to come into my study; I asked him to show me how to enlarge the photo on my web-site. He showed me, and magically, it was larger. I could, finally, see who it was. It was Donna. I became excited about the connection, once again, after twenty-five years. She was now in her fifties. She knew I was married and had a wonderful family. Because of the many postings on Facebook, it seems the world is connected, instantly. She did not want to intervene on a personal level, because she was also happily married. However, curiosity got the both of us, and we both wanted to know how we had progressed through the years. I told her about my careers and life in general and told her that I was writing a book, was looking at old photos for inspiration and had come across her teenage photo. Looking at the photo had brought back many memories, so I wrote a story about our experiences. I sent her the story about 'The Sacred Cove' of our teenage adventure and her appearance fifteen years later at the Ball Room dance.

She responded:

Oh Jay, what a wonderful love story, I've read it over and over again. Reading it made the years melt away and made me feel sixteen again; for that I thank you. What I remember most about you is your goodness and your eyes; I don't think there is another pair of eyes in the world like yours. To me, they looked into my soul. I remember sitting on the stairs, too; as for nibbling my ears, (to this day, I've never let anyone else do that ...I wonder if my subconscious knows they belonged to you). Why did I run away that day? My life at home was not good; I just couldn't take it anymore. That night in the cove, you made me feel safe and loved. It was something I had not felt since my mother died when I was nine. It's what I've searched for the rest of my life. Unfortunately, not everyone is you. The Ballroom meeting was truly a fairy tale scene; I was so happy to see you there, but as usual, we had to do the 'right thing'. One scene I remember is when I was in the hospital. I was very close to dying; although, I did not know it at the time. You walked into my room (did God want us to see each other, one last time?). I had you in my life then, for a short time. There is more to our friendship

than most ever have. It's been twenty-five years since
we last were in contact with each other. I'd love to
know what you are like now. Tell me what your life
is like, what your dreams are now; are you happy;
how did you find God? I want to know the adult Jay,
and I'll tell you about the adult Donna.

P.S. In my high school picture, the locket around
my neck is the one you gave me for my birthday.
I still have it; it is one of the many treasures I still
have of you.

One night in May, I Googled your name and
found you on Sound-click. I did not realize you
had responded, sorry. Looks like our sons are pretty
hip, themselves (by the way, Cameron has your eyes
and your smile!). I have a truly blessed life. When I
figure how to down-load pictures of my family to my
Facebook page, you can check out my brood. I would
love to have your CD's. If you want to keep in touch,
I will enjoy hearing from you.

Donna.

A DRESSAGE CHAMPION

Catherine, a Grand Prix rider with Olympic goals for herself, had a vision of a way to fund her journey toward training expenses and preparation for Olympic riding in dressage. The farm would become a means of supporting her goal. She already had won most of the local dressage events and had accumulated high points in the District and Regional Competitions.

Grand Prix is an international competition at the highest level of riding, in dressage. Competitors must work their way through increasing difficulty to an extremely high level of performance for both horse and rider. She had risen to that level and is continuing toward her goal of qualifying for the competition and representing Bermuda in the 2012 Olympics in London. Most riders are sponsored when they reach the top competitions. Some are left to foot the bill in the smaller, qualifying competitions, including registration and transportation for the horse but may get a sponsor if they qualify. Catherine's vision is to teach other riders to achieve higher levels in dressage, and in turn, she will be able to fund herself in those qualifying competitions.

During her competitions, the local equestrian club of which she is a member printed her results in their news-letter of each event. They sent these results out to everyone. Her results were so impressive that other dressage competitors in the club wanted her to train them and wanted her to help them find a suitable horse. Having worked with horses for so long, Catherine knew the importance of finding the perfect horse for a particular rider. She knew that she could find a suitable horse for anyone. The classification of breed is important, whether it is a warm blood, a horse from Hanover, Germany or a retired thoroughbred from Kentucky. "Horse people are funny people," Catherine says. She should know. It takes one to know one. She has been teaching for several years. In addition to being a qualified instructor, she has taught hundreds of riders over the years, including one Olympic-level rider.

Although she loves to teach riders, her real passion is training horses, especially in dressage. Dressage is a style of riding in which the trained horse performs complex movements in response to barely perceptible signals from its rider. She has a more elegant definition of the dressage. "Dressage is harmony between horse and rider. Most people, when you mention dressage, think of all the fancy steps. It isn't that. It's the respect, the obedience, the harmony, the bond between the rider and horse while doing certain exercises. Dressage, at higher levels, is like watching a horse do ballet to music. It's brilliant. It's phenomenal."

She spends months and months on basic training before moving on to a higher level. She says, "You can go faster, but when things fall apart, you always have to resort to the basics." She trains with her voice and her eyes, not with smashing palms or cracking whips. She claims that it is very rare that she ever loses her temper with a horse. "If you have to beat your horse to get it to do what you want, then it's not the right horse for you. It takes time, patience, a stern look and a strong voice to turn an inexperienced horse into a potential champion." She trains riders the same way.

Catherine on "Roy" Rolls Royce, a potential dressage Champion

TRIUMPH OVER TRAGEDY

Catherine and I decided we did not want to struggle through another winter. The farm had become too much to handle for only the two of us. We sold the farm in 2007, after enjoying that experience. God had blessed us and provided an opportunity for us to learn and survive. While living in Tennessee, we have never had to work for anyone other than ourselves. It was hard work, but what we accomplished was more than anyone could be grateful for. Our daughter, Jacqueline, was now married and moved to Nashville. Cameron was away, attending college. We purchased a smaller place that is only 3 acres. Catherine continues to train equestrian riders and their horses. I continue with my music ministry. I also began to do odd jobs in carpentry and painting, to help friends and to generate extra income.

Adversity came once again; this time it was tragic, unexpected and far more than anyone could have possibly imagined. On June 4th, 2009 I faced yet another storm in my life, but this challenge exceeded all others. Because of a freak accident, prayer, God's grace and major medical care were all that stood between me and the Great Beyond. I am confident I have evidence of the mighty power of prayer, because I had a miraculous recovery after a freak accident and being attacked by rare, flesh-eating bacteria.

A project in carpentry led to one of the most horrific events of my life. It started with my son's athletic consultant regarding requirements for college entry. He was a retired lawyer with an interest in helping high school graduates to get athletic scholarships. I agreed to pay for his services by doing projects at his house. I had much experience in painting because of taking care of my own home. Although I was an entertainer and hotel executive, over the years, I have enjoyed doing that type of work. It was something I had done during summer holidays after high school.

At the lawyer's home, I had completed one project, and the quality of my work was so appreciated, it led to another project. His wife asked me to build her a work bench where she could do copper sculpture, a hobby of hers. She suggested I use wood from left-over trusses piled in a field near their recently-built house. I went out to the field, that sunny June day, to examine the wood. When I lifted up the wood, there was a wasp's nest. I had disturbed it. I had jeans on and didn't realize one of the wasps had stung me just above my right knee. I was not allergic to wasp stings, and I went on with the day not thinking anything about it. Two hours later, while in the work shed putting the cut wood in order to build the work bench, I began to feel nauseated and felt a terrible pain in my leg. I left the shed and went to the main house to tell the owner I had to leave. The wasp sting pain would not stop. His wife suggested I rub ammonia on the sting, 'an old remedy her parents had used.' She brought out a gallon container from the pantry. I took it to the bathroom, soaked toilet paper in it and dabbed it on the sting. I decided to go home to lie down for a while.

At home after resting a few hours, the pain got worse, so Catherine took me to the hospital. In the emergency room the doctor looked at the wasp sting and said that he saw stings like the one I had throughout the summer. It was no big deal. I was given Benadryl and Demerol for the pain. He said the pain would go away, and I was released to go home. The only worrying sign that the doctor saw was a developing purple bruise near the sting site. However, it was a far bigger deal than either we or the doctor thought.

Back home, I continued to have severe pain throughout the rest of the night. Early in the morning, before day-light, the pain worsened. My son, Cameron, rushed me back to the hospital. By the time I reached the hospital, I was going into septic shock. Cumberland Medical Center, in Crossville, Tennessee, kept me for observation. Catherine called the hospital to find out my condition. At the time, they said, I was okay; however, they wanted to keep me for observation to find out what was causing me to go into septic shock. After a number of hours, a nurse called Catherine and told her that my organs had begun to shut down. I was in severe condition. I was put in the ICU. They discovered that a hole about the size of a doorknob had opened on the right side of my leg, just above my knee. They asked Catherine, had I arrived in the emergency room with my leg in that condition. Catherine replied, "The reason why he returned to the emergency room was because the pain from the wasp sting would not stop. When he left home, it was still just a purple pin-like spot. He came in earlier and the first doctor just looked at it and prescribed Benadryl and Demerol. He did not fully examine what else could be causing the extraordinary pain he was having."

What were they observing? Didn't my vital signs show something was seriously wrong? Why hadn't they taken my clothes off to examine my whole body? They only discovered my deteriorating leg after I was transferred into ICU. The condition of my leg was deteriorating rapidly, as was my whole body. These questions cannot be answered.

Richard G. Martin, Jr., M.D., F.A.C.S. General Surgery / Breast Cancer Surgery had just come out of a previous surgery. Because of his expertise and experience, he was asked by one of the examining Doctors to assess the situation. He had seen several cases similar to mine and said immediately, "This man is very sick; he needs to be transferred to a disease specialist right away." He called three hospitals, Vanderbilt in Nashville, Erlanger in

Chattanooga, and St Thomas, also in Nashville, Tennessee. I was now in critical condition.

(Approximately a year and a half later, I personally met Dr. Martin at the Fairfield Glade Conference Center. I did not know who he was until he introduced himself. He had been sitting on a bench watching his son play basketball. I had also come to watch my son play basketball. The bench was large, so I asked him if he didn't mind me joining him. He looked at me in amazement. He said, "You don't know me, do you?"

I replied, "Sorry sir, but should I?"

He answered, "I am Dr. Richard Martin. I know who you are, and I know all about your case." He proceeded to tell me of his involvement in my situation. After our intense conversation, his wife came from the pool area to where we were sitting. He was about to introduce me to her, but she already knew who I was.

Immediately, she asked, "Did he tell you what he did?"

I said, "Yes."

She replied, "His insistence that you be transferred may have saved your life."

She then left and headed back to the changing room, I guess. Dr. Martin and I sat and talked for quite some time while watching our sons. We talked about many other unrelated things. When he was about to leave I politely asked if he had a business card. I didn't ever want to forget this man.)

After the doctors had stabilized my situation; I was flown to St. Thomas Hospital by Life Force One, an air medical transport team. At St. Thomas, they rushed me immediately into surgery. At this hospital I was, eventually, diagnosed with Group A Streptococcal toxic shock syndrome. I had developed several serious infections. I had also contracted rare, flesh-eating bacteria in my right leg, and it was now entering the upper part of my body.

The bacteria eventually infected several other parts of my body. I had respiratory failure, acute kidney failure, blood clots, tissue rotting and bowel failure. There were so many other failures in my body, only a specialist doctor would understand.

(June 2, 2011 at the Fairfield Glade Assisted Living Center, the facility was having an appreciation day for care-givers, special speakers, and entertainers etc, anyone who had provided service at the center. I sang gospel songs and played music for the residents. The doctor and I had a conversation after introducing ourselves. He asked me how I lost my leg, and then asked if I was a veteran and now living at the facility. I told him I was an entertainer and how I had lost my leg. He told me that he had worked at St. Thomas Hospital and another hospital in Nashville for thirty years. He now lives in Indianapolis and was visiting. He said he had seen many cases of Streptococcal flesh-eating bacteria; it is deadly. "Many patients do not survive. You were lucky!" He told me of the many symptoms I have already described. I knew than that he was qualified and knew what he was talking about. I had been through it all.)

Things were not going well. The doctors told my wife and my four children that I had very little chance of survival. The family gathered at the hospital, waiting to hear the worst. The doctor returned to battle the odds, trying to save my life. I was told later that there were very tense moments. Most of the medical team said that I would probably not make it. The surgeon came to inform my wife. Catherine asked if there was anything more they could do. He said that if they amputated my leg at the hip and removed part of the bacteria that had entered just above the hip it would stop the spreading. She replied, "Do what you must do."

I had never been that sick in my life, and this was one of the worse situations that I have ever experienced. All my life, I have helped people in churches and hospitals and the disabled, doing benefit concerts for people who had lost their homes in fires or whose homes were damaged from storms and others who had to have major surgery. I never thought I would be in the same position as others I'd helped. Had the Cumberland Medical Center doctor diagnosed this extraordinary pain correctly from the beginning, maybe my leg might have been saved. It was concluded by the investigative medical doctors that no one will ever know what caused this extraordinary illness. As one doctor said, "He is lucky to be alive."

Another said, "His survival is a miracle of God."

To me, the greatest thing about what happened to me is that tragedy made my faith stronger. When the community heard what had happened to me, people stopped all over Cumberland County and began to pray, I didn't know this until I got home, much later. The news travelled all over the country and abroad...so many were praying for my life to be spared. People I didn't even know heard about my situation and prayed for me. They had heard through word of mouth and by email from Pamela Bracket. She is the sister of my son-in-law, James LeCroix, the husband of my youngest daughter, Jacqueline. James and Jacqueline live in Nashville, approximately twenty minutes from St. Thomas hospital where I was admitted. James and Jacqueline visited me daily after work and kept Pamela informed by phone. She lives in Crossville, Tennessee, ninety minutes out of Nashville. I'm thankful for Pamela's contribution toward my recovery in the hospital. On a weekly basis, she kept my friends, family and fans updated on my progress through the internet. She asked for their continued prayers. The people who did not have internet service were informed by the ones who did have service. The concern of everyone grew tremendously as many signed up for her weekly report.

Church announcements and phone chains were also used as a means to keep people informed. One couple in particular, from my Bible study group at the Crossville Church of the Nazarene, Howard and Sherrill, were so impressed with her updates that they kept them. When I rejoined the Bible study group, they showed them to me. I was in very critical condition the first few weeks fighting for my life. My whole body was going through trauma; so her emails began a few weeks later, after I slowly began to recover.

June 30, 2009, Pamela's first email:

I love it when I can bring you good news, and today is no exception. Jay's white cell count is NORMAL! Praise God! The infection is gone. They did have to give him a pint of blood. The doctors found a kidney stone. His kidneys were not functioning as they should. They were producing urine, but were not filtering the blood. He is trying to talk, although the words are not very clear because of the valve from the tracheotomy.

(It was more frightening to see my throat cut open for the tracheotomy; singing was my life, the thought of losing my voice was worse than losing my leg!)

He has made it very clear that he is upset, because he wants to go home to Crossville. He doesn't understand why he has to stay there in the hospital. The doctors call it ICU Syndrome. But considering everything he has been through, who could blame him for wanting to go home?

He is beginning to feel phantom pains from his missing leg; however, they will greatly diminish over time, although he could feel them for the rest of his life.

(No kidding! It's been two years since the surgery and daily it feels as though someone is cutting off my foot. It's a horrible feeling of helplessness. Sometimes it feels as though I have an itch on my knee; I want to scratch it, but it's not there. Other times it feels like a painful lightning throb going down my 'invisible' leg.)

It is still going to be a long recovery, but with God's grace, Jay has the spirit and fight in him. He WILL make it.

As for the benefit concert last night organized by Bob and "T" Shurmur at the Palace Theater, it was a great success. To see many people from the community, both performers and listeners, come together for Jay and his family, touches the heart. God's people really do care.

(When I was released from hospital, "T" Shurmur visited my home and presented me with a photo album of the concert. The photos were taken by a professional photographer, Walt Riches. I was overwhelmed to see the capacity audience in the photos and the entertainers who performed that evening. Some I had performed with at many other benefits and there were others I had not even met yet. "T" told me that, after hearing of my tragedy, she had to do something, and the best she could offer was her talent. Within two days, she had the line-up of entertainers who wanted to help. She said, all the musicians wanted to help a person who was always there when someone called. The city donated the Palace Theater for the performance.

Earlier in the year "T" and I had both performed in a concert called *Malt Shop Music and Memories* produced by Diane and Dennis Donald of D-Square Productions. It was a benefit for the high school students at Stone Memorial High School. I had performed in a few of their other productions, including the *Rat Pack Show,* living the memories of Frank Sinatra, Dean Martin, Sammy Davis Jr. and Peter Lawford.)

July 1, 2009, Pamela's second email:

Wow! What a way to start the month! I have many good things to share tonight. Jay has started physical therapy, and he is doing really well. I am not sure what they are having him do, but James says Jay is doing really well with many of the exercise techniques shown to him.

(Weeks later, my hip at the amputation area had healed. However, my organs, and body were still very weak. I was in recovery for many more weeks. I was so weak I could not lift a spoon. I cried one day when the Physical Therapists came in to start therapy by lifting my arms. There were two of them at all times, two therapists for my arms and hand coordination and two for my remaining leg and body exercise. At the beginning of my exercise routines I thought I'd never be able to function again. I did not want the therapist to see me struggle and be tearful, so before they left my room, I asked them to tie exercise bands around my bed. At night when everyone was gone, I was all alone. In the stillness of the darkness, I slowly exercised my arms at my own pace. I did this every night. One day, the arm and hand therapists came in, and I told them, "Watch this." I could finally lift one arm. I cried in jubilation. This was the beginning of my confidence and persistence to become strong once again. God was providing the strength. The therapists came in daily and showed me other exercises. I was making slow but steady progress.)

Pamela continues... Now for the bad news: They are beginning to find blood in his stool. They had to start giving him 2 pints of blood a day to make up for the lost blood.

(At this point of recovery, I kept complaining about an abdominal pain. I told the doctor of the pain. He told me I had been through major surgery, and my organs were still healing. It was a normal development. The pain persisted. For me, it was not normal. Eventually, I insisted that the doctor must have a thorough look. The doctor finally arranged for me to have an x-ray. They found that my colon was severely damaged. They had to cut my stomach open and operate, leaving a long scar. My stomach took weeks to heal. After that surgery, when the leg and body exercise therapists came in, the leg exercise was not as painful as the arms, but when they tried to move my body, I had severe pain in my stomach. The therapist thought that I was making excuses not to exercise my body and urged me to work harder. One day, when the nurse came in to change my bandages, I asked the therapists not to leave. I wanted them to see the condition of my stomach. The doctors had not closed the length of the cut. It was a new procedure, to allow the stomach to heal from the inside out to the surface. When the Physical therapists saw the open wound, they gasped in shock. Finally, they realized that I was not trying to avoid effort. They apologized and understood why I could not move my body without pain. They told me, that in many other rooms, patients just did not want to exercise. I told them, "I can assure you that I want to do as much exercise as I can to get out of here.")

July 7, 2009, Pamela's third email:

> *Good morning friends. Hope this finds that everyone had a safe and happy July 4ᵗʰ holiday.*

(July 4th, I had been scheduled to perform for the Veterans at a rally in the city of Crossville, Tennessee. For the past couple of years I had been invited to entertain as a tribute to the soldiers of the past and present. Families were there, also, to honor their lost ones. The soldiers were fighting for their lives and the freedom of others, I, too, was fighting for my life and for obvious reasons, could not be there.)

> *Pamela continues.. .I have great updates to brighten your day. Jay is now off pain medication, as well as all antibiotics. As of yesterday, he has not been on dialysis in about a week. This is not to say he is off completely. His kidneys are beginning to function, but slowly.*
>
> *They have inserted Jay's feeding tube; although, he is getting irritated because he wants to eat and drink on his own.*
>
> *Jay has not lost any of his faith. James said that, when he was there to visit tonight, Jay had been up, reading his Bible. Before James and Jacqueline left for the evening, he asked them to have a word of prayer with him. Oh, what a wonderful thing it is to be a child of God!*
>
> *The interest in his updates is growing tremendously. If you have anyone else that would like to receive my emails, feel free to give them my email address.*

COMPETENT AND COMPASSIONATE MEDICAL TEAM

The nurses at the St. Thomas hospital could not understand why I had such a good attitude after this tragedy. I said, "I did not lose my faith in God." When I could not do personal things by myself, the nurses were extraordinary. To be a nurse, in my opinion, is a gift from God. They were so caring and understanding. I had four to five extraordinary young graduates from Vanderbilt University taking care of me in shifts, daily. They were overseen by their University instructor and the Head RN, at St. Thomas Hospital. They were competent and compassionate. They administered the medications with gentleness and caring. Whenever I had an accident in bed, they immediately took care of me. After they did what they had to do, they left the room and headed to the next patient. As soon as they left, it happened again. I had no control over the functions of my body. I apologized every time. They always replied, "It is okay, Mr. Fox; you can't help it," and calmly cleaned up, once again.

Many times, they shared their personal goals and concerns in their life. The Head RN on one shift shared with me her interest in wanting to be transferred into Surgery. She was very interested to experience other areas in the medical field. Another young nurse was interested in becoming a pediatrician, working with new-born infants. An experienced nurse had a difficult decision to make. She loved working at St. Thomas but was needed back in Alabama to care for her aging father.

There were times when they were all there in my room together, administering medications and monitoring vital signs. While they were sharing their stories, I asked them to circle my bed and hold hands while I prayed for them, asking God to open doors for them and to comfort their concerns. They did this gracefully and reverently, without hesitation. I was bonding with the medical team which was taking care of me. They felt great coming into my room; I was sharing the 'Light.'

I had to learn how to eat again. A nutritionist spoon-fed me like a baby, at first. I had the most beautiful lady nurses taking care of me; it was easy to be cooperative, even though I had to start training my body functions all over again.

Before I got to the eating and the exercising stage, I spent hours semi-conscious because of the drugs I was given and my body and mind's reaction to the trauma I had experienced after the major surgery, I was kept in a coma for several weeks; I had hallucinations. The doctors had to put me in a coma state to operate and to relieve pain; it was now beginning to wear off. Some of the comments and stories about what my family told me that I had done were hilarious. Some I do not recall ever saying, others, that I personally remember, were very real to me. For example, Catherine said that I told her, "Get me that pineapple over there."

She asked, "What pineapple?"

I replied, "Are you drunk? Don't you see it over there on the table?" The table, of course, had several items but no pineapple. It was very upsetting for her to see me in that state of mind; she had to leave the room. It is difficult to act as though everything is normal when the person you love is not.

I have given the following stories titles so you can follow them easily. These stories were later evaluated by the hospital

Research Coordinator Mitzi Baker from Vanderbilt University. I have been asked to assemble a collection of my experiences to be used by medical professionals in the treatment of others who have experienced hallucinations during coma and recovery. You can log onto www.icudelirium.org; at this site you'll find research on patients, delirious after coming out of a coma.

The Terrorist Training Exercise

The Twin Towers, in New York City, before
and after the terrorist attack.

Shortly after I came out of the coma, my daughter, Jacqueline and my son, Cameron, visited me. They visited as often as possible, to keep me company. When they had to leave me, not realizing my disoriented condition, I asked if I could leave, also. Jacqueline, of course, said, "No, Dad, you have to stay until you're much better." I begged them to take me with them. She replied, "Mommy is coming to visit; she'll explain." When they left, I thought that they were just kidding and had just gone around the corner. They would be back soon; I was certain. As I sat there in my wheel chair, the wait for their return became longer and longer. It became very lonely just sitting, sadly looking out of my door. I could see nurses at their stations, going about their normal business. Suddenly, there was a lot of commotion. My room was facing the emergency entrance where patients came in for treatment. I could hear several sirens outside. Coming through the glass doors were several people on stretchers with severe wounds. It looked like they had been in a war or explosion. If you saw the television coverage on September 11th, 2001, of the terrorist attack on the Twin Towers in New York City and all the commotion after the buildings began to crumble, you surely can imagine what it must have been like in the hospital emergency rooms in that area. This is what it seemed like to me as I watched.

In my present situation and condition, looking out of my room, I saw everyone who worked in the emergency room drop what they were doing and begin to help. I was impressed with the swift help given by volunteers; even the same doctors who had helped me survive had slings on their arms. I said to me "This can't be right. Even the doctors and nurses are injured!" One of the doctors was outside my door, so I asked him to come in and tell me what was going on. He told me it was a training exercise. He said, "We do training like this once in a while; in case there is a real terrorist attack, the hospital will be prepared to handle the situation." His words relieved my concerns. He asked if I'd like to join in on the exercise, as a patient. He made arrangements, and I was taken out of my wheel chair and laid onto a stretcher. They quickly rolled me down a corridor where I was put into an X-ray machine. During this exercise, the trainer was taking photos of all the procedures, and logging the timing. Timing was crucial, because it meant life or death to actual patients in a terrorist situation. After I participated in the exercise, the doctor thanked me and wanted to give me an award as a memento.

I was later told, by the Research Coordinator assigned from Vanderbilt University that this whole event was a hallucination, and it really did not occur. A few weeks later, while still in recovery, I asked my Clinical Case Manager, to find the training room at

St. Thomas hospital where they recapped all the procedures and had lectures to improve their emergency procedures which I had imagined. They cooperated to help me connect with reality. I requested that they find the training instructor who had taken photos. Had anyone found the photos, this would have proved it was a real exercise. No one could find the nurse who I said had taken the photos. This effort was all to no avail. They could not find a training exercise on their books or anything to support my vivid memory. I was certain that it actually happened. Then I wondered, how could I have come up with such a logical event? The story seemed so real. It was all a part of my brain's recovery process.

The Death of a Patient

Another incident of similar nature occurred while I was in my room in another area, called H-pod. I sat in my room, looking out, seeing what was going on. I could see there was a young nurse, crying uncontrollably. I was told by a nurse in my room, that she had just lost her first patient. When her patient died, the young nurse became very emotionally involved. She had taken care of the patient for quite some time and had begun to like the person. When the patient died, she took it very hard. She had been grieving for quite some time. I could see from my room that the hospital had arranged the patient's room for the family to come and pay their last respects before his body was taken to the morgue. The nurse was crying so much that others were trying to comfort her. Across the room was the Head Nurse; she was rather unsympathetic. She told the young nurse that she should not have become so attached.

I then watched the young nurse disappear and return with a small flask of whiskey to calm her nerves. Where she purchased it, I surely don't know; I'm sure the gift shops don't sell liquor. She hid it under her service station. After having a few hits, she became a little tipsy. She told the head doctor she was going home and started to proceed toward the door. The doctor, realizing her condition, immediately called Security and told them not to let her drive and to send her back to him. She came back, and the doctor took her into the office to comfort her.

Back in my room, I asked the Head Nurse to come in. I told her not to be so confident about herself; one day it could happen to her. I told her, "Surely you all can't be so detached from patients when you're in the care business, helping them to get well. Suppose the family had been coming down the corridor and heard you tell the young nurse she should not have become so emotionally involved?" The Head Nurse got very upset at me and stormed out of my room. Again, I was told this story was a hallucination, and not real. But for me, they were real, and it was upsetting to be shown proof they were not so.

There were many other hallucinations I experienced during this recovery period, they seemed absolutely real to me, and yet, they were not. Some people take a long time to regain their sense of reality after experiences like these. I had a follow-up evaluation several months later at Vanderbilt Medical Center, in Tennessee. It was in the Research Department. I was tested for two hours on my emotional and psychiatric condition.

The Research Associate, who tested me, commented on my remarkable recovery. I gave him my documentation of the visions and experiences that I recalled, and titled it "Triumph Over Tragedy." I did not want to give it to him before my examination because I did not want it to influence his evaluation. He said he would pass it on to his superior Dr. Ely. Dr. Ely received the documentation and called me a week later. He told me, he was very impressed that I had taken the time to document my experiences. He said it supports their research with other patients who had similar hallucinations and delirium.

THE LITTLE TASKS

This story is true. After I came out of the coma and I began my therapy, the Care Pastor from our District office, Pastor Richard Reed and his wife Carolyn came to visit me. We had a wonderful visit and prayed together. The East Tennessee District Church of the Nazarene, District Superintendant, Pastor Ron McCormack and his wife Karla also came to visit. They presented me with my Ministerial Certificate. I became so emotional that my eyes were too blurry to see it. I had completed my ministerial courses before this tragic accident.

When they left, the therapist came in to teach me to wash myself. I had to start all over again, learning simple tasks, because I had become so weak. This was the first time in weeks after the operation that I was able to sit up and look into the mirror. When I looked, I could not believe the appearance of my face. For the first time in my life, I had a long oriental-type of beard. It was a long, lonely string of gray curly hair hanging beneath my chin. The skin of my face was very tender and smooth, and ordinarily, I never let it grow more than a whisker. It had been two months since I had last been able to shave, so you can imagine how I looked. I told the nurse, "I can't believe I look like this in front of people." My face was very thin, like death had already hit me. I asked her to get me a razor, immediately. She offered to shave me; I accepted. She did a fair job; however, I finished doing it the way I liked it, not a blade of hair would be missed. This was my first experience of getting back to doing all the little things.

Later that evening, Jacqueline came for a visit. Entering the room with her were her good friends Jessie and her husband, Gary Hook. Jessie happened to be a hair stylist. She gave me a hair-cut. Jacqueline's friends, Tanner, Ashley Sean stopped by on other occasions.

Edmund Fox and Llewelyn Hall, two of my very best friends from my first group, *The Bi-ington Whistle,* had called from Bermuda several times. The contact from family and friends felt like a life-line back to recovery. On several occasions I received a call from a fellow ministerial student, Dan Miller. He and I had prayer and talk about our ministry.

What a way to lift a sick man's spirit. I began to feel good again in spite of losing 68 lbs. Before this accident, I stood at 6'3", I was a healthy 195 lbs; at this point, I was only weighing 127 lbs.

All of my children were affected strongly by what had happened to me. My youngest daughter, Jacqueline, told me the most moving story. It brought tears to my eyes. I became very emotional. She told me, that, while I was lying in bed, motionless, she stood on one side holding my hand. Cameron, my son, stood on the other side holding my other hand. Catherine, James (Jacqueline's husband) and my two eldest daughters, Julie and Rebecca, also stood by the bed.

Jacqueline told me that, as she held my hand, a flood of memories came over her. She remembered when she was a little girl in Bermuda; she and I traveled across the harbor by ferry to go shopping in the city of Hamilton. I took her to fancy restaurants to teach her how she should be treated by a guy when she was old enough to date. Every Christmas Eve was our special day to shop for gifts. As we walked on the busy sidewalks, I held her hand. As the palm of my hand gloved hers, I gently rubbed my thumb on hers. At the bedside, in the hospital when this thought hit her, she collapsed. She suddenly realized that there was no movement from my thumb. I was asleep, but she had feared differently. Tears begin to trickle down my face as I think of that moment. I realize how serious it was for her. My accident happened in June, 2009 when Jacqueline was six weeks pregnant. She was due to have her first child in late December or early January 2010. How awful it would have been to lose her first child because of the shock of possibly losing her Dad. I triumphed over all the challenges and survived. Jacqueline had her first baby boy on January 4th, 2010. She named him Matthew.

The LeCroix Family
Jacqueline and James celebrate the birth of Matthew

On the other side of the bed stood my son Cameron; he, too, faced important decisions. He had recently graduated from high school and had been awarded an athletic scholarship. He was to attend Rend Lake College in Ina, Illinois. I had been Cameron's first basketball coach. I was also a baseball coach, and we traveled from county to county. He had made the All Star team, and I was one of his coaches. He and I have a very close father and son bond. Friends and family told me he was very emotionally torn. The possibility of losing his Dad so suddenly and tragically left him with many questions. What would he do? How would he handle the loss of his father? Would he not go college, at that time? Would he have to stay home and be with his Mom? He pondered for a while and decided that going to college is what I would want him to do, and Catherine fully supported his decision.

Cameron and his high school sweet-heart Destiny

Julie and Ernest had given me three grandchildren, Ajai, Alia, and Aidan. She was about to have her fourth child when I was hospitalized. She knew the child was a girl; her name was to be Ariah. Julie was terrified of losing her father. She is my first child. She had experienced travelling to England with me at the age of four. She saw the joy on my face when I met my father for the first time. They all flew from Bermuda to be by my side. She arrived in Tampa, Florida and joined Rebecca for the drive to Nashville, Tennessee.

Julie and Ernest Peets

Rebecca, too, was facing concerns. The previous year, all the family had gathered and treated me to the best Father's Day celebration since I had my children. We spent the day in Nashville, at the water park. I went down the water slides like a little kid and had a great time with the grandchildren. Later, we had dined in one of the finest restaurants in Nashville. When her vacation was over, Rebecca had returned to Florida. After her return, I received a horrible letter saying she never wanted to ever see me again. I was in shock. The memories of her childhood had flooded her mind. The divorce of my first wife, her mother, overcame her thoughts. She felt that I had abandoned her when she was a little child and did not love her. I guess, seeing how I was having so much fun with the grand-children made her think of the days she had missed. She was only four at the time of the divorce. She recalled our last conversation in the letter. She had realized, after my hospitalization, that she could lose her father and be left with the thoughts of what had been said and what had never been resolved.

While I was still in hospital, she had a remarkable revelation. Through much prayer and support from her husband and very close friend, Michelle, she gave her life to Jesus Christ. She began to attend church regularly. Before that experience she had very little faith in God. Now, she had put herself into God's hands.

TRANSFER TO BAPTIST HOSPITAL

Dr. Bonau, the Consulting Physician at St. Thomas hospital, was feeling very confident that I was now finally recovering. He was preparing to have me transferred for further physical therapy. He sat beside my bed and talked for awhile. He described what I had gone through, the amputation of my leg, my organs failing, and said that I had been very near to dying. He told me he believed in prayer, but it was a miracle that he was sitting there talking to me and that I was recovering well. He held his head between his hands and slightly bent away from me, in thought. I could feel within my heart that he was thinking that he wished he could have done more, but I knew he had done all he could. "It is up to God to do the rest," I thought.

After eight weeks at St. Thomas Hospital, I was transferred to Baptist Hospital also in Nashville, Tennessee, for further physical therapy. Each day I had a rigorous schedule, and each day I progressed, getting stronger and stronger. I started by taking six steps with the support of the double hand bars. I soon transferred to a four-legged walker. I progressed to twelve steps, then twenty-four, then up to ninety. I'll never forget the therapists at the Baptist Hospital; they were very competent and compassionate. Marty, before leaving his shift, had taken me for a stroll in my wheel-chair outside to feel the sunshine on my face, something I had not felt in 10 weeks. Sam, another therapist, kept my mind occupied with games, weight lifting and balance. Unexpectedly, after two weeks, I was in severe pain; blood began to seep through my left leg above my knee. It was the area where they had taken a skin graft to cover the wound where the doctor had to amputate at the hip. I returned to my room. The following morning, I tried again; I could not take one step. I could not even lift the exercise weights for my arms which only weighed one pound each. At that moment, I began to sob; I asked the therapist what was happening to me. I should be progressing not regressing. She reminded me that I had been through a major ordeal. I returned to my room. This time, it was horrible. It finally hit me, what had happened. I looked down, and finally, finally, finally realized the severity and trauma my body had gone through. For so long I had blocked the full extent of the tragedy out of my mind.

All alone in my room, I cried uncontrollably for two hours. The therapist came in my room, (listen to this!) she was not the regular therapist I had been working with for the past two weeks. It was Saturday; she was covering for someone who was off that day. She had very light blonde hair, and was dressed differently than the others had been. She saw that I had been crying and was concerned about me. She proceeded to say, "It's okay to cry; sometimes God allows us to cry, to relieve the stress and pain we face in our lives." She continued, "Trust in Him; He will bring you through all this."

At that moment, I could not believe what I was hearing. God had given me many messages in the words of the songs I had recorded. I realized that I had to listen to the words that He had inspired me to write and understand them, myself. I asked her not to leave until she received a copy of my CD entitled *After the Sunset*. This CD was my first Christian music release. Three of the songs on the CD were written and composed by me. I had asked Catherine to bring a box of my CDs to the hospital, so I could hand out them to everyone who had taken care of me. I knew it was not necessary, but in my heart, I wanted, in some way, to show my appreciation for their care and to witness my faith. One nurse said that she had taken her CD and listened to it in her car during her lunch break. She said, "It felt like I had spent an hour of meditation in holiness and solitude."

One of my compositions, *Victory Feelings*, has a line in it that says:

Trust and believe, for God is our Friend.

The Physical therapist, in her caring words of encouragement, had made me realize that, in my own songs God had not only inspired the words to bless others but also to glorify Him and to bless me as well. She was grateful for the CD gift and left. Was she an Angel with a message? I never saw her again. I never even asked who she was.

I took a quiet moment alone with God in a prayer. I prayed. "Dear Lord, our Heavenly Father, continue to give me strength, do not let Satan discourage me, and take away my trust in you." After my prayer there was a wonderful peace that came over me, and I fell into a deep sleep.

The next morning, an orderly came with a stretcher to transfer me to the x-ray room. The doctor had ordered an x- ray to see what was causing the pain and blood seeping through. At first, he thought it was fatigue because of my rigorous therapy schedule, but in the x-ray, they found something different. After the x-ray, I made a joke to the examiner. I said, "Well, am I going to live?"

She replied, with a serious voice, "I'll let the doctor tell you."

That answer alerted me with concern. Upon returning to my room, Dr. Bomboy arrived at the same time. The first words out of his mouth were, "Have you called your wife? You have a blood clot." When he asked, if I had called my wife, I thought he meant that I did not have much time to live. While I was being monitored during the past several weeks, they had been concerned that I could possibly get a blood clot. They had told me it could be very dangerous. I was really scared.

The doctor's statement was good news and bad news in the same sentence. He actually wanted to know if I had called my wife to make arrangements to take me to see the plastic surgeon, Dr. Oslin. I had forgotten that Dr. Bomboy had made previous arrangements for me to see him because I was progressing so well, before this last incident. Dr. Oslin's office was back at St. Thomas Hospital. He had performed the skin graft on my hip after my leg was amputated. The plastic surgeon needed to give the okay for the healing success of the surgery. Dr. Bomboy then said "We'll need to put you on Coumadin to clear the blood clot." You can imagine how I felt about his first comment, before he clarified what he had said.

Each day and night the RN came and put a needle into my side to administer the blood thinner. The blood clot was eventually cleared, and the pain in my left leg stopped.

The plastic surgeon, Dr. Oslin, gave me thumbs up on the healing process of my hip and reiterated how much I had improved, over all. He was one of the doctors, in the beginning, who had thought I was not going to make it. I was glad to have surprised him and the others. Actually, Dr. Oslin came to visit me several times, even on his days off. He often would stop by my room to see how I was progressing. After examining the amputation area, he stayed awhile longer and we talked about our athletic sons. I bragged about my son's State Championships in Track & Field, and he bragged about how well his son played Football.

We enjoyed our conversations; however, he now told me, sadly, that his son had been seriously injured in a game and could not play again. I could sense he loved his son very much and was proud of him. One morning, Dr. Oslin was out jogging and stopped by my room. It was his day off. He still had his running gear on. It was during the time I had severe pain in my abdomen.

He thought it was just a digestive problem, so he went out of his way to a grocery store and brought me a pack of peach flavored 'Activia.' It sure was delicious. However, the pain was more serious than indigestion! After insisting a doctor investigate thoroughly, I had major surgery again. My colon was found to be severally damaged. The only way to rectify the problem at the time was to have a colostomy.

After stabilizing my condition, I continued to do my therapy and was finally released after four weeks.

DEATH OF MY MOTHER

While recovering from the shock of suddenly losing my leg, another sad occasion was unfolding. My mother had come from Bermuda to visit me in Tennessee. A few months before, my mother had been admitted into the hospital for severe respiratory failure. She had battled asthma for years and had been in and out of hospitals for treatments. Her condition was very severe; her heart was failing. She had been released from the hospital, but the doctors had advised me, while I was in good health, that she only had a few weeks to live. At our home, Catherine and I took care of her daily. We did everything we possibly could to make her last days comfortable.

When I was suddenly admitted to the hospital, Catherine's attention was turned toward me. My mother was then taken care of by Catherine's wonderful friends. Catherine was able to travel back and forth from Crossville to St. Thomas Hospital, in Nashville. It was a three hour drive, daily. She had little time or attention for anything else.

Friends later told me that Catherine never gave up hope that I would recover. Her faith in me knew that I would overcome all challenges in this fight for survival. It was my trust in God, her strength and the love of my family which kept me from focusing on the severity of what had happened to me. I was told that the shock of my loss would hit me later, and it did.

My daughters, Julie and Rebecca, returned to Florida, taking my mother with them to ease the burden on Catherine who was focused on my recovery. While Mother was in Florida, Rebecca and her mother, Helene, continued to care for her. Julie, Ernest and the children returned to Bermuda. Julie had the baby a few months later and named her Ariah.

After a few weeks in Florida, my mother was admitted to intensive care once again. She soon passed away of respiratory and heart failure. I did get to speak to my mother over the phone a few times before her passing. She did not realize the severity of my condition.

The family took her passing very hard. Even though I was in recovery myself, I had to comfort my family. I told them we had all done the best that we could, and Mother knew that she was very much loved by us, all. I also assured them that the battle was finally over for their grandmother. 'Singer' was a few days from turning 80. She had had a busy existence, full of love from the family she had made. After her long and active life she was at peace. She had found her calm after the gale force winds of her life.

Jay and Mother Illyria 'Singer"

RECOVERING AT HOME

Like the people celebrating their survival of the terrorist attack in New York seven years before, I was grateful to be alive, but my life had changed in ways I was only beginning to discover. I was finally released from the hospital, September 11th, 2009. I am now at home in Fairfield Glade, Tennessee. I use a motorized wheel chair provided by Kathy and Nathan Humble and a four-legged walker to get around. Again, friends and neighbors rallied around Catherine and me and provided medical equipment that I would need. One couple, Jim and Carlene Everett, even provided a hospital bed with exercise bars. It was a long time before I could drive again, but, thankfully, now I can go where ever I choose.

The first time, I got in the car with my wife, and I drove down the road, just a little. It was so easy and natural. While driving down that road, I started shouting, "I...N...D, I...N...D." Catherine, asked, "What are you saying?" I guess she thought I was going nuts. I was expressing myself in joy, because I felt independent, once again. Remember, for three months in the hospital and for the months that had followed after my release, I had lain helpless and dependent on others. Now I felt free!

A few days before that drive, I had sat at the dining room table, reading all the cards and letters that had arrived. Tears had begun to fall from my eyes and down my face. The mail had come from senior centers, churches, businesses and from people whom

I didn't even know. I had not realized how many people I had touched, over the years, through my music ministry. The cards and letters had begun while I was in the hospital and continued after I returned home.

While I was recovering in the hospital, I asked my wife to pick me up a box of thank-you cards. After she got them for me, they just sat there, on my side table. My intentions were good, but I just could not write. The box of thank-you cards eventually came home, with all my other belongings. At that moment, sitting at the table, I began to pray and ask God for His direction as to what to do about this situation. There were just so many cards and letters to answer, one by one. I felt overwhelmed by the task. My first thought was to call the local news paper and arrange for a press release. The meeting was arranged, and the reporter came to my home. This was so much better than trying to hand-write and mail hundreds of personal cards.

There was much talk going around the community about what had happened to me. All everyone knew was that I was critically ill in the hospital. Many thought that I had gotten bitten by a poisonous Copperhead snake or Brown Recluse spider. I felt that I needed to clear those thoughts of the public, because they needed to know what had really happened. I took the opportunity to add to the press release to thank all the community for their prayers and their support for my family. The article came out in the paper a few days later.

That was my idea for the answer to the situation, but God had something bigger in mind. When I received His answer and direction to my prayer, it was as though He was standing right in front of me saying, *Go, an tell them in person.*

"Wow!" I thought to myself. "That makes sense." Many times in our lives, we don't wait for God to answer. We do it our way and find out what He wants us to do the hard way. Like a good Father He lets us try and fail as many times as we need until we are finally ready to listen. I now could drive, and it was almost

Thanksgiving. Many Senior Centers and Churches around the area had Thanksgiving dinners, and many Churches had larger congregations during that time. I had a lot to be thankful for; perhaps I could share. I called several churches, large and small, telling them I'd like to come and thank their congregations at a service. Several others, I traveled to meet with the pastor. Harvey LeCroix, James' father, drove with me. Many of those churches were delighted that I would take the time to come and give my testimony and to thank the people, in person, and the dates were set.

Another avenue I could use to thank the people who had blessed me with their support during my struggle for my life was to visit Senior Centers. When I was Music Director at the Mayland Church of the Nazarene, I had arranged many gospel singings. I invited many people from the community to attend. The singings led to many other singings at the Mayland Senior Center, next door, Easter, Thanksgiving and Christmas dinners and several other benefits for them.

During these concerts, I met an elderly Lady named Helen Gore, a jewel of the community. She became a very good friend and fan of my music. Whenever I appeared at a singing, she came up to me and requested her favorite song "I Know Who Holds Tomorrow". I, of course, sang it for her. Everyone knew how much she loved my singing and speaking engagements. It inspired so many.

One day, years ago, I was travelling past Mrs. Gore's house on route to the church to prepare music for morning worship; standing outside of her home was Charlotte Mullikin, a very close friend of Helen. She flagged me to stop. I did, and then rolled down my car window to hear what she had to say. She told me that Helen Gore was very ill and would I come and have prayer with her. I was concerned as she had become such a good friend and did not hesitate. Everyone knew that I was a man of God, so I believed it would be appropriate to do so. Inside, I met Roy Welch who also was a very good friend of Helen. He was giving her water and attention. Mrs. Gore was lying on the sofa in the living room. I quietly knelt beside her and asked how she was feeling? She replied "Not so good!" We, Roy, Charlotte and I gathered around Mrs. Gore and prayed; asking for God's mercy and healing. I gave my regards to Helen, Charlotte and Roy, then left.

Ten years passed, and I received a phone call from Charlotte telling me Helen Gore was about to celebrate her 100th birthday. She was ninety the day I prayed with her. I was invited to be her special guest and share our stories and, of course, sing her favorite song. The celebration was held at the Mayland Senior Center, and how wonderful is this? Over one hundred people showed up. Praise God, for He is still in the miracle business. It is said that God determines who walks into your life...it's up to you to decide who you let walk away, who you let stay, and who you refuse to let go. As I write, she is still going strong.

Charlotte Mullikin was now the President of the Center; I asked her when would be the best time to come to the Center to thank the people who had prayed for me and sent cards and letters? She, of course, was delighted. She then asked if I could also sing at their Thanksgiving dinner. At the Center, the people were in tears to see my recovery, and I was nearly in tears to see the caring in their eyes.

My next stop was the Fair Park Senior Center, another large group in the Crossville community. I arrived at the Center and requested to see the director; her name is Peggy Houston. I entered her office, and she invited me to have a seat. I had sung at their Pioneer & Heritage Day each year for the past few years. Two years in row, I produced radio commercials which played over the air to promote the event. However, a month or more before the annual event was to happen, I had my accident. I told Peggy I was sorry that I was not able to be there to sing and be part of that fundraiser. She clearly understood and, obviously, knew that it had been impossible for me to be there. I had been busy staying alive.

At that moment, sitting in her office, it was almost as though a light had gone off. You know the light that clicks on in your head when you have a great idea! She said, "It's not too late; let's put on a Christmas Concert.

Excitement in her eyes, she then said, "We'll put it on at the Palace Theater and call it 'A Christmas Celebration'." The Palace Theatre is a newly-refurbished Historic Theatre in down-town Crossville, Tennessee. At the Palace, they have had many other fund-raising events. I have sung at many of those events, such as the Miss Senior Tennessee Pageant. I told her she had to book a date soon, because time was running out. They may not have an open date. I left the Center, and she went to work making the arrangements. I continued to make my visits. Over the following weeks, I travelled in a radius of more than 100 miles, and shared my testimony. Peggy later contacted me and told me that the Palace Theater was all booked for performances during the holiday weekend; she then proceeded to say, "Thursday, December 10, is available." I told her to go ahead and book that date and maybe the afternoon as well, for a matinee. I knew, if God had a hand in it, we would have a full house. She replied, "Let's just book the night, since it is a short time to advertise." I immediately put together a group of singers, which included: Joennen Kettler, a wonderful female vocalist, *The Tennessee Gospel-Aires* and my trio, *Greater Faith,* Betty Green, Charlie Brewer and myself. The concert was an overwhelming success.

The Palace was full, and several people were outside who could not get in due to the building capacity. I shared my testimony and once again thanked the people for their support and prayers. God had found a way for me to return all those cards and letters without writing hundreds of thank you cards. All I had to do was ask Him.

THE TRIP TO FLORIDA

The following summer of 2010, I went to Florida to visit Rebecca. Julie had returned from Bermuda and came to Florida with the grandchildren for a vacation. When I arrived the Sunday of that week, Rebecca and I attended her church together. As we sat and listened to the message, we had an incredible feeling of bonding; I could hear her singing softly along with the songs which were sung by the praise and worship group. I was so impressed by her voice, so I moved closer to hear her voice, attentively.

At that moment, her hand and mine clasped each other. There was a burning sensation, as if God was bringing us close together for the first time in years. We both felt that burning moment as our hands clasped, and tears began to flow. This special moment was something that was long overdue for both of us. She was now thirty-three. I had only travelled to San Diego, California once during the time she lived there with her mother. I saw her several times after she moved to Florida, but the distance still had made it difficult to see her often. She had felt abandoned. Now we were joined once more.

That week, while watching the grandchildren playing in the park, we had a long father and daughter talk. She talked of her childhood after her mother took her across to the United States to California. The story was horrific, and my heart began to sink. My worst nightmares had come true; she had had very bad experiences. I began to understand why she had become so bitter toward me. I knew in my heart, something had to have gone wrong. I had never given up on her, despite her bitterness toward me. I always told her that I loved her and always would.

For her, I was not there enough during those childhood days. I had not been there in person to protect her. We were thousands of miles apart. I could not be there when she needed me, even though I desperately had wanted to be.

Our tragedies brought us together; we both were given a second chance....God intervened for us and made the connection possible for us.

While visiting her that summer, something else incredible happened to me. The family spent the day at the local YMCA pool. Julie and Rebecca took the task to watch over the grandkids while they were swimming; Rebecca suggested that I sit by the pool and watch Mycah, her son, my grandson. He was practicing for an upcoming swim meet. While watching Mycah, I began to edge myself deeper and deeper into the pool, sliding down each step. For months, after my tragic accident and the loss of my leg, I was scared to death of going near a pool, thinking that I would drown. I was terrified that I would just sink to the bottom.

I live five minutes from a wellness center near my house. They have an indoor pool; however, I never had had the courage to go for a swim. As I got deeper into the pool, the water was now up to my neck. Mycah finished his practice laps and swam over to where I was. I said to him, "I can't stand the fear anymore; I'm going in all the way." I then said, "If I go to the bottom, just grab my arm and pull me out. But if I float, leave me alone to swim." I pushed off the last step, to enter a deeper section. Because I only had one leg, my balance was one-sided; my body spun over. I, eventually, caught my balance and began to swim. The grand-kids came running over to watch.

They were shouting, "Pop, Pop! Go under the water. Go under the water." I was still not sure if I could or not. However, I did try and was able to dive and swim half the length of the pool. Julie captured this moment on film and later posted it on Facebook. I reflected back to that moment, "Just think. A few months ago, I was near death." It was another exciting achievement for me after my recovery. I learned that I could still swim. Inside my mind, I screamed with excitement, like finding that I could still drive even though I only had one leg.

For people who do not understand the fear of having a disability, I, as well as many others, feel as though many of our abilities have ended; however, God has a way of revealing that we can still do things. As a disabled person, I now began focusing on things that I can do, rather than the things that I cannot do.

My son made a comment, (all in good thoughts, of course) and my answer sums it all up. He said, "Dad, I can beat you in basketball now."

I replied, "That's okay! I'm now going to take up kayaking."

I can no longer jump and run to play basketball, but I can use my upper body to paddle a kayak, and I can still swim.

What I can't do no longer matters Cameron will have to work hard to beat me at what I can do!

THE CONCERT

I travelled nearly a hundred miles to a small church in another town to share my testimony. After the service, the church gave me an offering toward my travelling expenses. This was totally unexpected. I introduced my son, who had travelled with me that morning. He received a warm welcome. I told him later, "See what happens when you trust in God."

Since I knew the offering was a gift from God, I was going to continue to trust in him. My plan was to reinvest the gift and rent the Fairfield Glade Community and Convention Center for one night. I wanted to gather the huge portion of the community that I thought I could have missed during my church and senior center visits. I arranged a Gospel Concert and called it "Triumph over Tragedy." I told my mentor, Pastor Richard Reed of my plans. Pastor Reed is mentor and Care Pastor of all our Pastors and Song Evangelist on the East Tennessee District Church of the Nazarene. He said, "That is sure a step of Faith." That it was.

When the evening of the concert came, I arrived early to make sure the room was prepared and the sound system was perfect. It was rather slow in the beginning, as people started to trickle in; I began to have concerns and doubts entered my mind. My thought was, "Is this idea mine, or is it God's? Surely," I said, "If this is God's plan, then it will be a success." As the concert time got nearer, an influx of people came from out of nowhere.

The Convention Center began to fill, rapidly. I used my walker and went around the room to personally greet as many people as I could.

God had put several hundred people in front of me to share my testimony and to glorify Him. I truly believe that is how I came out of a critical time of nearly dying. Prayer intervened. That is when I began to recover. I believed that faith saved me. God never tells you his plan; it just happens.

I haven't written any music since I was hospitalized, but I still plan to. The last song I released was: *Amazed,* long before I got sick. I was very fortunate to write the song, because I had just finished studying the Book of Mark, in the Bible, which talks about God's healing power. Now, I've experienced that power personally. Here are a few lines:

He can move a mountain; He can calm the sea.
He can walk on water, He can comfort me.

Along my journey, I have made it through the storms of life to become the character that I am. As I grow and mature in Christ-likeness, it is evident that Christ's character is being transformed in me. My concerns for the care of others, the passion I have as a Sunday School Teacher, improving my knowledge of Scripture, my lifestyle, and sharing the gospel in song have become very dear to me. My every thought and action as a person is part of the tapestry of integrity of my heart. I've learned to live with purpose and meaning, beyond my own interest and abilities.

As a Song Evangelist of the Gospel, the goal is helping to bring people into the body of Christ by presenting Christ's offer of free salvation by grace through faith. Each of these Truths is essential for equipping believers to share their faith effectively.

I'm amazed that so much has happened in between learning how to play the guitar and becoming a professional entertainer, a hotel executive, a Song Evangelist and, now, a Licensed Minister of the Gospel, in the Church of the Nazarene.

I continue to serve the community as a Lion, at the Fairfield Glade Lions International Club, in Tennessee.

Remember, God loves you, no matter who you become. Seek Him first, and remain faithful, for He alone can bring Triumph over Tragedy!

This is my testimony in Scripture

I waited patiently for the Lord, and He inclined unto me and heard my cry.

He brought, me up, also, out of a horrible pit... and set my feet on a rock and established my going.He hath put a new song in my mouth.Even praise unto our God: Many shall see it and fear.and they shall trust in the Lord. Psalms 40:1-3

For Recordings of Jay, make money order for $13.95, this includes tax & S/H, out to: Jay Fox, Mail to: 163 Drew Howard Road, Fairfield Glade, TN 38558

J.D.K. FOX Group of Companies

Orpheus Sound Recordings
Orpheus Publishing
Manchester Music makers
Tree Top Productions
163 Drew Howard Road
Crossville, TN 38558
jayfox.fox290@gmail.com

Easy listening CDs

Signature
Reflections
Island of Paradise
More than Ever
Something Special
Christmas Classics

Gospel Music CDs

After the Sunset
It's My Desire
Greater Faith featuring Jay Fox
Jay Fox "Live in Nashville"
He Calls Me Son

Recordings available on CD

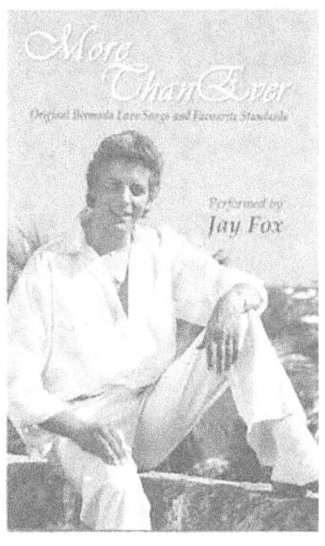

Gospel & Easy listening CD's

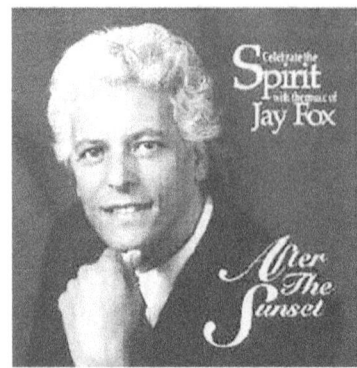

Ariah

Cameron my son, and grand-children; Ajai,
Aidan, Alia, Ariah and Mycah.

The LeCroix Family James, Jacqueline and Matth

A tragedy happened, and then came the greatest gift of all. Life.

Matthew LeCroix

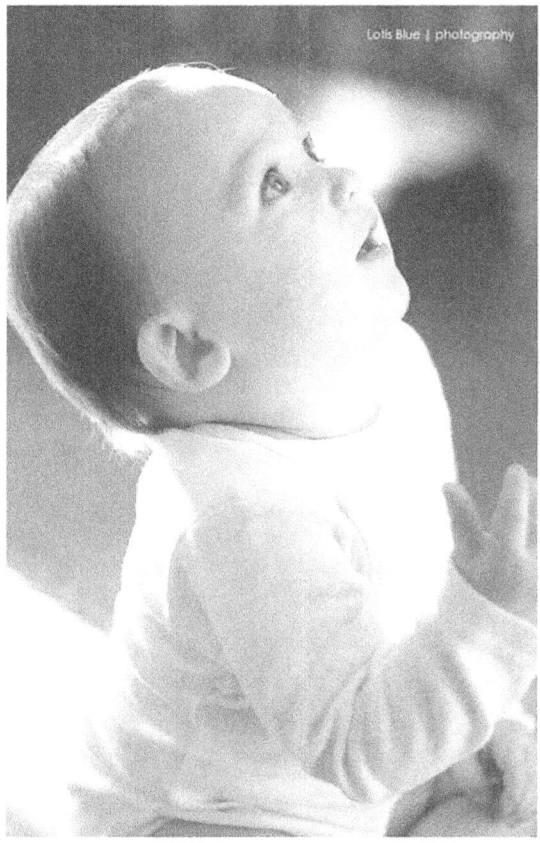

"Thank you, Lord for saving my grandfather."